Is It Well with Your Soul?

In troubling times everyone needs a way to comfort their souls.

Bill Peters

Is It Well with Your Soul?

Acknowledgments / Dedication

Initially, I would like to acknowledge Jesus Christ as my Lord and Savior and the Holy Spirit for their saving presence in my life.

Special thanks to Pastor Bob Sharpe for sharing technical expertise in bring this effort to its conclusion. Thank you for the editing work of Darla Partridge who made this effort so much better and for Angela Mantzey for her original and thoughtful work on and design of the book cover.

I also want to share my greatest appreciation and love for my wife Candy Peters without whom I would never have been able to accomplish what I have been able to in the writing of this book.

"I Love You Candy."

Contents

Preface 3

1 Death Comes Unexpectedly 7

2 Angel in Blue 21

3 Evil and Heroes 35

4 Heroes, Kings, and Chess 47

5 Surrounded by the Enemy.................. 65

6 Red Sky Warning 79

7 Are We Without Remedy?.................... 91

8 Hold On, A Message of Hope!............ 105

9 Is It ME or HE 119

10 The Excitement of Jesus.................. 137

11 The Supremacy of Jesus 145

12 Is it Well With Your Soul? 157

Preface

I don't know about you, but as a Christian I watch what is happening around the world and especially in the United States of America and I feel brokenhearted. It seems that everything good and moral and ethical is being turned on its head. Hate at the speed of the internet seems to be the rule of the day. Nothing is exempt or protected from the vicious attacks. It seems that if the right person or group is offended then changes must be made. This kind of hate seems to grow every day.

In January of 2019, following the "March for Life" in Washington D.C., the largest annual pro-life march in American history, a group of Catholic high school boys became the focus of ridicule and hatred simply because they were standing in the wrong place at the wrong time. A false narrative was quickly spread by the "Mainstream Media" which exploded across the internet and social media that these young men were racists of the worst kind and they had been threatening a Native American. Within 24 hours, additional video showed beyond a doubt that these young men were in fact the victims and had done nothing wrong, but that didn't matter they were mostly white teens, from a Catholic high school. Their crime was that they had participated in a pro-life march and were wearing baseball caps that displayed their support (MAGA hats) for the President of the United States.

With the 2020 Covid-19 virus pandemic hitting the nation and the world, the Christian group Samaritan's Purse deployed one of their emergency field hospitals to New York City which at the time was screaming for doctors, nurses, medical beds and other medical assistance. But when Samaritan's Purse set up their hospital, they were greeted by the Mayor of New York who said that he was troubled by this charity's understanding of human sexuality. He was also going to have people on hand to make sure that the Samaritan's Purse staff did not discriminate against non-Christians. This displayed a hate and disrespect for what Samaritan's Purse stands for.

Dr. Albert Mohler the President of The Southern Baptist Seminary, said this during his "Daily Briefing" on April 2, 2020 regarding New York's dislike of the Samaritan's Purse hospital; *"In its own way, New York City wants the hospital, but it doesn't want the Christian ministry behind it. It desperately needs this field hospital, but it doesn't want the hospital being brought by Samaritan's Purse. But just consider this for a moment. It really doesn't have any choice. It turns out that in many cases, the only organizations able to help are those Christian organizations that are ready to help precisely because of an extension of their Christian mission. They want Christian doctors and nurses to come to New York City, but they only want the doctor and nurse part not the Christian part. But no one seems to be asking the question, why are they going? Because the answer to that question is they're going precisely because they are Christians."*

In 2019 the state of New York passed the deadliest abortion bill in the United States of America. The new law allows for the termination of an unborn life up to and including the baby's due date. What was worse, at least for me was seeing the video announcing the passage of the law in the state legislature and the cheering that followed. I can't truly understand what is so gleeful about a law that allows for the murder of defenseless unborn American citizens. Yes, I said murder! That is because scientifically, we now know that life begins at conception. I do not intend for this to become a diatribe against abortion, but I say this to show just how depraved our society has become, and it shows no sign of stopping.

The Christian faith is now being pronounced by some in Federal elected office as a disqualifier for a judgeship on the Federal courts. It seems that nothing is unethical if it accomplishes what you want. Personal attacks, whether the facts are true or not are okay in order to take out your target. And who are the targets? Christians, conservatives, people that support the right to life, people who believe that marriage is between a man and a woman as described and created by God, not the supporters of gender choice. Those people who believe in law and order are also potential targets.

As I read and watch these vile things going on around me, I just want to cry, yes, real men cry. The breakdown of our society into an anything goes society is not only heart wrenching but so very destructive. As a Christian I understand these things because I and every other Christian have been warned: *"If the world hates you, you know that it hated Me before it hated you"* John 15:18. But on a reality level it is still tough to take. The constant negative drumbeats of hate against the things that I believe and try to stand for can wear a person down.

When I get down and turn to the Lord, I wonder if I am really that down. Is it that bad? I have not had my life threatened for what I believe, at least not yet. I have not lost a full-term baby that had been healthy for nine months and then just died. Then my mind drifts to the song "It Is Well With My Soul" Horatio G. Spafford, a man who had suffered great loss, yet through his faith in God was able to write those incredible words. I wonder if it is well with my soul. I have put together this collection of messages into book form in the hopes that they might be helpful to you and help you to ask "is it well with my soul" and I hope you will be able to answer "It is well with my soul."

1 Death Comes Unexpectedly

There are times that people have to deal with uncomfortable topics. This chapter is one of those times. Many years ago, when I was a young police officer, I rolled to the scene of a fatal traffic accident. What had happened was that two women in their early 20's were driving fast ahead of another car in which one of the woman's boyfriends was driving. They were having fun; I can only imagine that the two women were laughing about what they were doing, when the car entered a curve for which they were traveling too fast. The car rolled over, and the passenger was killed. When I arrived, the driver was sitting on the curb in total shock. Think about it; one minute the friends are laughing and having fun, then in a split-second two lives changed forever! One life ceased to exist and the other was likely mentally scarred for life. That event remains as real and vivid in my mind as when I first saw it over 40 years ago.

Think about what has been occurring across the nation and around the world with the Covid-19 virus and all the political unrest. So many people have been affected by the illness in a personal or relational way. The same is true regarding all the riots and unrest that have occurred across the Nation. Family and friends have died. Families and friends have been forced to be apart. Society was shut down; millions lost their jobs and so many people around the world are afraid that the world will never get back to some type of normal.

Have you ever seen the movie "*Pollyanna*"? Even if you have not seen the movie, you have probably heard someone referred to as being "pollyanna-ish" for being unrealistic, overly optimistic, and refusing to consider negative possibilities.

This 1960 Disney movie stars Hayley Mills as the little orphan girl Pollyanna Whittier, who is sent back to the United States to live with her Aunt Polly after the death of her missionary parents. Pollyanna's aunt, Polly Harrington (Jane Wyman) essentially owns or controls almost everything in the town of Harrington, even the church. For most of the movie Aunt Polly considers Pollyanna a nuisance to be tolerated (barely) as a "charitable" gesture to her deceased sister, Pollyanna's mother. Karl Malden plays Reverend Ford, the minister of the town's only church. Aunt Polly practically dictates Reverend Ford's sermons for him, "suggesting" the texts that he will preach from, and even the general tone that each sermon will take. From the examples we hear in the movie, it is clear that Aunt Polly's idea of a good sermon is pure hellfire and brimstone. Reverend Ford preaches at length about how death comes unexpectedly, and how we sinful humans will find ourselves judged by an angry, vengeful God and cast into Hell for an eternity of suffering. Wholly missing from his sermons is any mention of God's love for us, or of the saving power of Jesus Christ, whose death on the Cross provides salvation for sinners and allows us to appear before God in the pure perfection of Christ rather than in our own sinful nature.

As a Pastor and Chaplain, the sudden finality of death is usually in the back of my mind. A number of years ago while I was working for the California Department of Forestry and Fire Protection (*CAL FIRE*) a man I knew died in a traffic accident. He was a Chief Officer for *CAL FIRE*, his name was Bryan Zollner. I had worked with Chief Zolner during my time as the Information Officer for the San Bernardino Unit of *CAL FIRE*. Chief Zolner had moved on via promotion to northern California and while driving to work one morning, his vehicle reportedly hit a patch of ice on a mountain road. The car went over the side and Chief Zolner was killed.

And how many times over the past years have crazed gunmen attacked innocent and unarmed people and children killing them suddenly and without warning. These actions; The Las Vegas Shooting, the West Texas shooting, the Gilroy Garlic Festival shooting, the Thousand Oaks shooting, the Stoneman Douglas High School shooting. sadly this list is much larger and could go on and on. But in each and every one of these terrible events, the cause was pure evil. Genesis 3:5: *"For God knows that in the day you eat of it your eyes will be opened, and you will be like God, knowing good and evil."*

1 Corinthians 5:13: *"But those who are outside God judges. Therefore "put away from yourselves the evil person."*

3 John 11: *"Beloved, do not imitate what is evil, but what is good. He who does good is of God, but he who does evil has not seen God.*

When I ran a search of the word "evil" in my Bible study software for the New King James Version, I received over 500 verse locations. God thinks that it's a problem or He probably would not have mentioned it as much. However, you probably won't hear much about evil because people who don't believe in God do not want to have that discussion.

Some years ago, one Sunday after church, my wife was advised that the husband of a friend that she had worked with she was a Nurse Executive had died suddenly. This man had been informed that he had prostate cancer and leukemia, but they figured that he had more time than just to the next weekend. And of course, at times like these, the "why" question starts being asked. "Why did they have to die? Why would a loving God allow this to happen?" Well let's look at a couple of verses that might provide a bit of understanding. Deuteronomy 29:29: *"The secret things belong to the LORD our God, but those things which are revealed belong to us and to our children forever, that we may do all the words of this law."* The simple general meaning seems to be this: What God has thought proper to reveal, he has revealed; what he has revealed is essential to the well-being of man, and this revelation is intended not for the present time merely, nor for one people, but for all succeeding generations. The things which he has not revealed concern not man but God alone and are therefore not to be inquired after.

Death comes unexpectedly. I experienced this in 2017 and I will let the words from the memorial service for my best friend Chuck Pruitt explain how I felt.

"When a good person dies, family and friends gather for many reasons. Life has touched them with deep grief, and they need one another's company for their own comfort. Just to be together, to look in friend's faces and see the common expression of hurt takes away the loneliness of their feelings and draws their hearts together in the blessed healing that men and women can do for one another." So says William B. Rice.

This is true for me as well. Many times, the person being remembered is not a lifelong friend of the Pastor. In this case, Chuck and I had been friends since we were around 13 years old, having met at church. Our common bond was sports, which we played together as often as we could. Bowling, basketball, softball, football, mostly of the sandlot variety. As we grew and got that precious driver's license, it meant numerous trips to Huntington Beach during the summer.

We had trials and separations over the years but came back together as good and best friends during the last seven years or so. What made Chuck's departure from earth so stunning for me was that he and his wife Bonnie were in this very church for Easter Sunday and we were laughing and joking around. About 24 hours later, Bonnie was calling me to tell me that Chuck had died from a sudden and massive stroke and was now with the Lord. I can tell you this, it is with great relief that I stand before you and know that Chuck is with the Lord. That is a fact that we should all be happy about.

I would now like to quote from Psalm 103: 8 -17: *"The LORD is merciful and gracious, Slow to anger, and abounding in mercy. 9 He will not always strive with us, Nor will He keep His anger forever. 10 He has not dealt with us according to our sins, Nor punished us according to our iniquities. 11 For as the heavens are high above the earth, So great is His mercy toward those who fear Him; 12 As far as the east is from the west, So far has He removed our transgressions from us. 13 As a father pities his children, So the LORD pities those who fear Him. 14 For He knows our frame; He remembers that we are dust. 15 As for man, his days are like grass; As a flower of the field, so he flourishes. 16 For the wind passes over it, and it is gone, And its place remembers it no more. 17 But the mercy of the LORD is from everlasting to everlasting On those who fear Him, And His righteousness to children's children."*

I shared a few of these verses when we interred Chuck's ashes.

What a great weekend to be able to have Chuck's memorial service, since it was Memorial Day weekend and Chuck as a naval veteran, is worthy and deserving of this recognition.

You know, one of the reasons the Psalms are quoted so often is that they provide a beautiful verbalization of many of the things that we think and feel yet may not be able to find words for. Never is this so true than at a time like this. We are at the same instance saddened at the loss of Chuck, but we are joyful in the knowledge that he is with the Lord. In Psalm 103 we see that in all of His dealings with His people, the Lord shows Himself to be merciful and gracious. He guides, protects, and provides for every step of the way when we allow it. But there comes a time when God has to deal with us, but as we see in verse 10, God does not give us what we deserve, He gives us mercy. The penalty for our sins was paid by another at the Cross of Calvary.

Just as a human father, God watches us with loving understanding as we struggle through the trials of life. As David says in verse 15, we are like grass. Grass here translates as wild grass, seasonal grass. We as grass are born, we grow, and like flowers of the field we stand out in our life for the things we do. But in verse 16, we find that the wind brings the end of the season for wild grass, so death brings an end to our earthly existence. However, we need not fear the wind of death, because the mercy of God is from everlasting to everlasting for those who know Him, and God gives that to his children's children.

We also see this in a different light in 2 Timothy 4:6-8: *"For I am already being poured out like a drink offering, and the time has come for my departure. 7 I have fought the good fight, I have finished the race, I have kept the faith. 8 Now there is in store for me the crown of righteousness, which the Lord, the righteous Judge, will award to me on that day--and not only to me, but also to all who have longed for his appearing."*

Chuck fought the good fight. Many times, life seems more like a fight than it does anything else. We get knocked down and God helps us back up. We face health concerns, many times an uphill battle, but we go on, just as Chuck did. We face grief and we need help from God to continue. Chuck has finished the race; Chuck has run his course. He has lived his life here on earth and now it is done. For many of us, Chuck's race of life was ended too early. Chuck and I still had Tommy Burgers to eat and conversations to have. But this happens to all of us. Scripture describes for us in many different places that life is a race and we are to run it with all our might. There is a finish line and that line is death. James 1:12: *"Blessed is the man who perseveres under trial, because when he has stood the test, he will receive the crown of life that God has promised to those who love him."*

Chuck certainly persevered. Even after his first minor stroke, Chuck stayed as busy as he could. He was a large part of his grandson's life. Candy and I and the church were happy to see Chuck and Bonnie here on what would be his last Easter Sunday. It is a bit unworldly to know that the last church service that Chuck attended was here and the last message he heard was mine. What an honor from God to be the last to share His Word before my lifelong friend. This is how I closed my message on Easter Sunday; "Because Jesus was God, no one could have killed Him here on earth without His permission. When you look at all the torture and abuse He sustained, how could a mortal man have survived just to get to the cross? Jesus was and is life itself and it would have to be His self that relinquished that human life here on earth. Isn't it great that as saved Christians we also have access to eternal life with Jesus Christ, the one who defeated evil, sin, and death." Rossiter W. Raymond wrote "Life is eternal; and love is immortal; and death is only a horizon; and a horizon is nothing save the limit of our sight."

Now let's take a quick trip through the Bible and read about life and death.

Job 14:14: *"If a man dies, shall he live again? All the days of my hard service I will wait, Till my change comes."*

2 Samuel 14:14: *"Like water spilled on the ground, which cannot be recovered, so we must die. But God does not take away life; instead, he devises ways so that a banished person may not remain estranged from him."*

John 11:25-26: *"Jesus said to her, "I am the resurrection and the life. He who believes in me will live, even though he dies; 26 and whoever lives and believes in me will never die. Do you believe this?"*

Romans 8:12-13: *"Therefore, brethren, we are debtors — not to the flesh, to live according to the flesh. 13 For if you live according to the flesh you will die; but if by the Spirit you put to death the deeds of the body, you will live."*

The Scripture declaration that in the midst of life we are in death never had a more striking illustration than in a thunderstorm on the Hudson, where a young officer of the Twenty-Second Regiment, militia, was sitting writing a letter in the YMCA tent. There were several long tables in the tent, at which the men were accustomed to sit and write.

16

Corporal McDonald and ten others sat at the table nearest the entrance. The young corporal had arranged to celebrate the close of the tour of camp duty on the following Saturday by getting married, and when the tent was struck by lightning, leaving its mark on the floor and furniture, he was writing to his fiancée. The letter was complete, and its last words were: "Yours until death." The date was to follow, but when the expectant bridegroom had written "State Cam—" the flash came and the pen stopped. The tour of duty was over—taps had been sounded—the lights were out. The best way to be ready to die is to live with reverent fidelity to duty. None of us ought to leave anything undone for last hours which may never be consciously known to us. (Author unknown)

Now, I don't mean to be morbid, but I have struggled with this notion of how quickly our earthly existence can end since I arrived on the scene of that fatal crash more than 40 years ago.

Since we cannot know the time or place when we might be called from this world, how can we be prepared? Well what we need is life insurance for eternity, and everyone knows who the agent is. Jesus Christ by His sacrifice on the cross for our sins purchased a group life policy with His blood for anyone who will believe in Him and invite Him into their hearts.

Is It Well With Your Soul?

So what is this eternal life insurance policy? It is of course SALVATION!

The steamer *Central America,* on a voyage from New York to San Francisco, sprung a leak in mid-ocean. A vessel seeing her signal of distress bore down toward her, and the captain of the rescue ship cried, "Let me take your passengers aboard now." But it was night and the commander of the *Central America* feared to send his passengers away in the darkness; and, thinking they could keep afloat a while longer, replied, "Lie by till morning." About an hour and a half later the lights were missed. All on board perished, because they thought they could be saved better at another time (Author unknown).

Now is the accepted time; 2 Corinthians 6:2: *"For He says: "In an acceptable time I have heard you, And in the day of salvation I have helped you." Behold, now is the accepted time; behold, now is the day of salvation."*

However, not only is your salvation important, but also the salvation of all who have not come to Christ and been born again. Today is a call to attention for your salvation and to make you aware that you are also called by Christ to be concerned about the salvation of others.

Matthew 28:18-20: *"And Jesus came and spoke to them, saying, "All authority has been given to Me in heaven and on earth. 19 Go therefore and make disciples of all the nations,*

18

baptizing them in the name of the Father and of the Son and of the Holy Spirit, 20 teaching them to observe all things that I have commanded you; and lo, I am with you always, even to the end of the age." Amen."

We need to be on fire for our community. Just think about how many people you have known that died and were not saved. Perhaps some of them were thinking about it and just never got around to it. Well they will never get around to it now.

We need to be a light for God's salvation, remember 1 Peter 3: 15:

"But in your hearts set apart Christ as Lord. Always be prepared to give an answer to everyone who asks you to give the reason for the hope that you have. But do this with gentleness and respect."

I want to close with this story; A sick man turned to his doctor, who was leaving the room after paying a visit, and said: "Doctor, I am afraid to die. Tell me what lies on the other side." Very quietly the doctor said, "I don't know." "You don't know the man said? You, a Christian man, do not know what is on the other side? The doctor was holding the handle of the door, on the other side of which came sounds of scratching and whining, and as he opened the door a dog sprang into the room and leaped on him with an eager show of gladness. Turning to his patient, the doctor said, "Did you ever notice that dog? He has never been in this room before. He did not know what was inside. He knew nothing except that his master was here, and when the door opened, he sprang in without fear. I know little of what is on the other side of death, but I do know one thing: I know my Master is there, and that is enough. And when the door opens, I shall pass through with no fear, but with gladness." (Author unknown)

Remember the sermon in the movie *Pollyanna*, "Death comes unexpectedly." I urge you that if you are or have been thinking that you need Christ in your life, then delay no longer. The gift is free for the asking, won't you take Jesus up on His offer?

2 Angel in Blue

Did you know that in this life we need to have a remedy? For example, for sickness we need a remedy to recover and in some cases survive. I would like to share about a good friend whose wife died from cancer. I have changed their names out of respect for their privacy, but the story is true.

I also want to talk about Proverbs Chapter 31, verses 10 through 31. God wants men to understand the place that women share with them in God's Kingdom. In fact, King Solomon spent a good deal of time pondering the question of how and where you find the right woman. How indeed!

In my New King James Bible, this section of Proverbs is titled "Wise Women." As we read about wise women, I want to weave into the conversation praise for an incredibly special woman, Rebecca. Rebecca was married to a very good friend of mine. This chapter allows me to keep a promise I made to God and Rebecca as I was standing before her coffin; that promise was to keep her name and witness before people. Rebecca died from cancer on February 5, 2002. This is her God inspired message to me to share with others.

Is It Well With Your Soul?

Proverbs 31:10-31

10 Who* can find a virtuous* wife? For her worth is far above rubies.

11 The heart of her husband safely trusts her; So he will have no lack of gain.

12 She does him good and not evil All the days of her life.

13 She seeks wool and flax, And willingly works with her hands.

14 She is like the merchant ships, She brings her food from afar.

15 She also rises while it is yet night, And provides food for her household, And a portion for her maidservants.

16 She considers a field and buys it; From her profits she plants a vineyard.

17 She girds herself with strength, And strengthens her arms.

18 She perceives that her merchandise is good, And her lamp does not go out by night.

19 She stretches out her hands to the distaff, And her hand holds the spindle.

20 She extends her hand to the poor, Yes, she reaches out her hands to the needy.

21 She is not afraid of snow for her household, For all her household is clothed with scarlet.

22 She makes tapestry for herself; Her clothing is fine linen and purple.

23 Her husband is known in the gates, When he sits among the elders of the land.

24 She makes linen garments and sells them, And supplies sashes for the merchants.

25 Strength and honor are her clothing; She shall rejoice in time to come.

26 She opens her mouth with wisdom, And on her tongue is the law of kindness.

27 She watches over the ways of her household, And does not eat the bread of idleness.

28 Her children rise up and call her blessed; Her husband also, and he praises her:

29 "Many daughters have done well, But you excel them all."

30 Charm is deceitful and beauty is passing, But a woman who fears the Lord, she shall be praised.

31 Give her of the fruit of her hands, And let her own works praise her in the gates.

So, to start off, who is this virtuous woman? The word virtuous can be a little confusing. It is a Hebrew word that refers to honor or integrity. It is used of men of valor who are trustworthy in battle. Integrity is probably the best translation. *"Who can find a woman of integrity?"* It refers to character –

what she is inside, not what she looks like on the outside. She is a woman of strength. And even though she is the weaker vessel, she is made strong by wisdom and grace and the fear of God.

This is the same meaning used in the Character of good judges in Exodus chapter 18 verse 21: *"Moreover you shall select from all the people able men, such as fear God, men of truth, hating covetousness; and place such over them to be rulers of thousands, rulers of hundreds, rulers of fifties, and rulers of tens."*

So, it would follow that a virtuous woman is a woman of spirit, who has the command of her own spirit and knows how to manage the spirit of others, she is one that is pious and industrious, a help mate for her man. A virtuous woman is a woman of resolution who, having good principles, is firm and steady in them. Obviously, these women really are much more valuable than jewels.

God fearing women had a great deal to do with what made this a great nation. Remember, behind almost every member of the continental congress was a wife and mother, supporting the men, raising the children, and keeping the homes and farms.

One of the foremost women of Proverbs during the founding of the United States was Abigail Adams, wife of one President and mother to another. From her writings, we see a woman displaying many of the ideals of these verses.

On October 16, 1774 she wrote, "I dare not express to you, at three hundred miles distance, how ardently I long for your return.... And whether the end will be tragical, Heaven only knows. You cannot be, I know, nor do I wish to see you, an inactive spectator; but if the sword be drawn, I bid adieu to all domestic felicity, and look forward to that country where there are neither wars nor rumors of war, in a firm belief that through the mercy of its King we shall both rejoice together..."

On June 18, 1775 she writes to John, "The race is not to the swift, nor the battle to the strong; but the God of Israel is He that giveth strength and power unto His people Trust in Him at all times, ye people, pour out your hearts before Him; God is a refuge for us."

And finally, in a letter written on June 20, 1776 from Abigail to her friend Mercy Warren, "A patriot without religion in my estimation is as great a paradox as an honest man without the fear of God. Is it possible that he whom no moral obligations bind, can have any real good will towards men? Can he be a patriot who, by any openly vicious conduct, is undermining the very bonds of society? The Scriptures tell us "righteousness exalteth [sic] a Nation..."

From Proverbs verses 11, 12, and 23 we find that the virtuous woman is a devoted wife. She has her husband's confidence; she seeks his welfare. She does him good all the days of his life and hers as well. She works to enhance his reputation.

When Rebecca was in high school, she decided she wanted to be a police officer. But after she graduated, she fell in love with my friend. Her husband was becoming a police officer, so Rebecca took the position of a devoted wife, and later a devoted mother as well.

In verses 13 through 17 we see that the woman is a diligent partner. She pays attention to the needs of the family and the best way to provide for these needs. She is a willing worker, a good shopper and planner plus she has strength from spiritual and physical fitness. She is not one to sit and just work inside but wants to do the best she can even if it takes getting a bit dirty.

So too was Rebecca. As her husband advanced in his career, Rebecca worked part time outside the home and full time as a wife and mother. She kept herself physically fit even after two daughters. Rebecca was not above getting dirty if she had to. Getting the work done and without complaint was her primary objective. In her 20s, she began her relationship with the Lord, for whom she was devoted to and diligent in serving.

In verses 15, 21, and 27, our woman of Proverbs is a dependable mother. She is devoted to the needs of her family. She does not like to just sit and watch time idle by. She wants to be involved and working, accomplishing something. The woman of Proverbs knows that God did not send us into this world to be idle, because being idle makes us a good target for the devil. She is well groomed, organized, and disciplined. And as such is a good testimony for her children.

Rebecca was also like this woman of Proverbs in these areas. She worked for the needs of her family, she supported her husband, and she was always there for her daughters. She was involved; Rebecca was always doing something, either at home, church, or at work. She helped at school on a regular basis and coached her daughters' soccer teams.

However, it wasn't all Ozzie and Harriet for my friend and Rebecca. After their first few years together, they broke apart and divorced. I remember sitting with my friend as he struggled with what had happened, even crying together over the situation. But God won out and my friend and Rebecca remarried. For me it was a rare privilege to be the best man at both of their weddings. Following the second marriage, they both worked harder to create a union more like God had in mind.

It was during this time that Rebecca became like the woman of Proverbs in verse 26, doctrinally oriented and full of God's wisdom. Why is this important? Well, women face two tremendous forces of persuasion. First, they face the deceptions of Satan. Do you know why Satan worked to deceive Eve and not Adam? Satan knew that Adam had walked with and talked with God. Satan knew that Adam had seen with his own eyes the wonder of God creating. However, Eve had not seen these wonders from God. Satan knew that he could never confuse Adam because of what Adam had seen, but Satan felt that Eve was less experienced in these matters.

Women also face a satanically controlled system which has as its goal the destruction of home and especially motherhood. If you do not believe that, just look at the personal attacks that were directed at Karen Hughes, President George W. Bush's Chief Advisor during his first campaign and early years in the White House. Feminists from all sides attacked her as a bad example for women's success in business. She was the closest advisor to President Bush, and feminists were appalled that Karen Hughes would just leave this success and power for something as quaint and old fashioned as wanting to spend more time with her husband and son. What a victory for a woman of Proverbs. You can also see this in the constant attacks against First Lady Melania Trump, who tries to be faithful to her husband, her son, and her duty as the First Lady of the United States.

The second force has aided the first. This is the abuse of women by men. Man's mistreatment of women has made women ripe for the propaganda and humanistic ideas of the world.

As husbands we are told to care for our wives in two ways:

As Christ is the Savior of the Church, so husbands are to provide for their wives, not simply by putting bread on the table. This is not a Fred Flintstone thing. We are not just to arrive home from work with the paycheck, yell out Wilma's name and expect her to flop a big brontosaurus burger on the plate. We are to provide emotional, spiritual, physical, and mental support for our wives as well. This does not mean that a hearty hi how are ya every day meets those requirements.

The second way we are supposed to care for our wives, our children's mothers, is to love them as Christ loved the Church. That is a PRETTY INTENSE LOVE....... Here are a few questions to ask yourself?

Do I want for my wife what I want for myself?

Do I want to avoid for her the unpleasant things I want to avoid for myself?

Our lives and homes are filled with opportunities for us men to show our love and concern for the best part of our earthly lives. It was in these areas that my friend and Rebecca cemented their relationship and strengthened their marriage

Proverbs verse 31 is where Rebecca and the wise woman of Proverbs truly became one: *"Give her of the fruit of her hands, And let her own works praise her in the gates."* Remember, God places women on an equal footing with men. Not as modern feminists describe it, but equal before the Lord to receive His love, grace, strength, and redemption. As we live in God's plan and remain faithful to Him, God often rewards us. For Rebecca, that reward was the realization of her high school dream.

With her two daughters well established in school and past the formative years, Rebecca, at age 36, began her quest to become a police officer. But in this life things can be difficult and so was this quest. As she interviewed for a position with a Southern California police department, the Chief was naturally curious why she had waited so long to get into law enforcement.

She told the Chief of her dreams from high school and the importance of her marriage and wanting to raise her children the way she wanted. She now felt it was her turn to realize her dream. She was hired and given a date for the Police Academy. She had to miss that date when she was diagnosed with breast cancer.

As the next academy date rolled around, the Chief had some concerns about Rebecca being able to participate and successfully complete the grueling academy while undergoing chemotherapy. After another interview, he liked her spirit and determination and decided to let her try.

On the first day of the academy, following a really tough day, Rebecca asked to talk to the training staff. Having been there myself, I'm sure the staff was eagerly anticipating a weepy female coming in, head down and telling them that she couldn't do it and she was quitting. They were rocked on their heels when Rebecca told them of her situation but advised them not to worry because she had scheduled her chemotherapy treatments for the weekend so as not to miss any academy time. She also promised them that she would not fall out of physical activities and would remain current with her academics. She told them she expected no favors and the only reason she was telling them any of this was because her Chief ordered her to do so.

My wife and I were thrilled and proud to attend Rebecca's police academy graduation. She passed her probation and became her dream. Rebecca was a Police Officer. After about two years on the job, her cancer returned. She was forced off work for more treatment. Rebecca underwent the harshest regimen of chemotherapy that the City of Hope offered in an effort to rid her body of this killer.

Through this, Rebecca never complained. She continued to care more for her family and others than herself. Her faith never faltered; in fact, it became stronger. Once again, the cancer was driven from her body and in mid-2001, she returned to her patrol car.

In early December of 2001, the cancer returned with the vengeance of evil against the righteous. This time there was nothing medicine could do. But even as she lay in her hospital bed, the last night of her life, Rebecca was concerned for others, her husband, her daughters, and her God.

Rebecca assisted in the plans for her memorial service. She wanted to make sure that no one was inconvenienced. She also demanded that the service include two very special wishes:

That everyone attending be told that she loved God with all her heart and she did not nor should anyone else blame God for what had happened.

That an invitation be given for those who might not know God and wanted to give their souls to Him.

Remember verse 31 which says; "GIVE HER THE FULL FRUIT OF HER HANDS."

God did just that. Rebecca put Him first in her life and was given her dream.

Verse 31 concludes; "AND LET HER OWN WORKS PRAISE HER IN THE GATES." So they were. Nearly 500 people turned out to honor this incredible woman who,, at the age of 41, went to be with her Heavenly Father. She was praised without contradiction. It wasn't false praise for a friend who had died. It was praise for a woman who had lived in God and for God. And putting Him first was rewarded with her dream and the righteous praise of those who orbited around her. Rebecca was buried with her husband's Medal of Valor which he wanted her to have for her incredible bravery in facing this deadly illness.

I asked God on the February morning we laid Rebecca's body to rest that I be allowed to tell her incredible story. A story of bravery, devotion, diligence, dutiful service, dependability, and doctrinal soundness. Over the years since, I have been able to share Rebecca's story many times.

Do you want that kind of strength in your life? Do you want that kind of relationship with God? Do you want to be well with your soul? It's simple you know. If you are saved, pray to God for strength and guidance and have the faith to give God all of your heart and soul.

If you are not saved, you need to ask God into your life by believing in his Son Jesus Christ. Ask Him to forgive you of your sins and realize that Jesus Christ is the Son of God who died for your sins and my sins. If this is you, and you want Jesus to make it well with your soul, you can pray:

"Dear God, thank you for sending Your Son, the Lord Jesus Christ, to pay for my sins on the cross. Thank you that He died for me. I acknowledge that I am a sinner and that I cannot save myself. Please forgive me all my sins. I receive your gift of salvation by faith. Thank you for loving me enough to save me. In Jesus' name, Amen."

If you prayed that prayer, I want to congratulate you on becoming a new member of the family of God. Additionally, I have something to send you from In The Beginning Ministries that will assist you as you move forward in your new justified walk with Jesus Christ. If you would, I would like you to email me at itbministries@gmail.com with your mailing address and write in the topic line, New Child of God. And don't worry, your email and address will only be used to send you the information that I just spoke about. As you read on, I hope that you begin to see that it can be well with your soul.

3 Evil and Heroes

2 Timothy 3:1-5: *"But know this, that in the last days perilous times will come: 2 For men will be lovers of themselves, lovers of money, boasters, proud, blasphemers, disobedient to parents, unthankful, unholy, 3 unloving, unforgiving, slanderers, without self-control, brutal, despisers of good, 4 traitors, headstrong, haughty, lovers of pleasure rather than lovers of God, 5 having a form of godliness but denying its power. And from such people turn away!"*

Well we certainly witnessed this haven't we? Have you ever wondered what kind of evil inhabits a person that leads them to meticulously plan an operation designed to kill and maim as many people as possible, like the Las Vegas shooting on October 1, 2017 or any other mass shooting event for that matter? News flash... after every event as these, the world breaks into a tizzy wondering, speculating, and demanding officials find out what the perpetrator's motive was. Well I will tell you what their motive was: **IT WAS TO KILL PEOPLE.**

Evil does not need a motive; evil is a motive. And it is pure evil to execute a plan designed to kill as many people as possible. Proverbs 4:14-

17: *"Do not enter the path of the wicked, And do not walk in the way of evil. 15 Avoid it, do not travel on it; Turn away from it and pass on. 16 For they do not sleep unless they have done evil; And their sleep is taken away unless they make someone fall. 17 For they eat the bread of wickedness, And drink the wine of violence."*

How is Evil defined? **Profoundly immoral and malevolent.** And how is malevolent defined? **Having or showing a wish to do evil to others.** There's the shooter's motive defined.

Another thought that seems to surface during times like these is how could a loving God allow evil things like this to happen? The simple answer is because this is a broken and sinful world. Response; if God is all knowing, why would He allow Adam and Eve to sin if He knew what would happen? Good question. Are we responsible for our actions? God endowed humanity with free will, because it is only through free will that He can be sure of the love of humanity towards Him. However, with free will comes responsibility.

Listen to the beginning of *The Westminster Confession of Faith*, drawn up in the 1640s by an assembly of 151 theologians (mostly Presbyterians and Puritans) at Westminster Abbey. It is the standard of doctrine for the Church of Scotland and many Presbyterian churches throughout the world. Several other denominations, including Baptists and Congregationalists, have used adaptations of the

Westminster Confession of Faith as a basis for their own doctrinal statements. In each case, "the Westminster Confession is considered subordinate to the Bible." www.gotquestions.org.

Quote: "God from all eternity, did, by the most wise and holy counsel of His own will, freely, and unchangeably ordain whatsoever comes to pass; yet so, as thereby neither is God the author of sin, nor is violence offered to the will of the creatures; nor is the liberty or contingency of second causes taken away, but rather established."

Yes God knows what is going to happen, but it is mankind that is responsible for that happening. Cain had a choice with his brother Abel. Let him live or kill him. Cain chose to murder his brother. Mankind had a choice regarding the greatest evil ever perpetrated, the execution of Jesus Christ. Acts 2:22-24: *"Men of Israel, hear these words: Jesus of Nazareth, a Man attested by God to you by miracles, wonders, and signs which God did through Him in your midst, as you yourselves also know — 23 Him, being delivered by the determined purpose and foreknowledge of God, you have taken by lawless hands, have crucified, and put to death;"*

It is through evil and sin that God shows His Glory. It is through evil and sin that God shows his love and mercy. Romans 9:22-24: *"What if God, wanting to show His wrath and to make His power known, endured with much longsuffering the vessels of wrath prepared for destruction, 23 and that He might make known the riches of His glory on the vessels of mercy, which He had prepared beforehand for glory, 24 even us whom He called, not of the Jews only, but also of the Gentiles?"*

God will always allow a person to choose their own way, to choose what they will or will not do. But as we have seen from the Apostle Paul, eventually you will become hardened against the things and ways of God. Paul tells us in verse 22 that while God is long suffering, eventually those vessels (humans) that are determined to sin will be prepared for destruction.

There are several types of evil that exist on and in the earth. One is Natural Evil, which is what happens through natural disasters. Remember, the earth was also cursed at the time of Adam and Eve's sin. Romans 8:22: *"For we know that the whole creation groans and labors with birth pangs together until now."* In fact, the Covid-19 pandemic would be, I believe, a Natural Evil.

Another evil is Moral Evil which dominates humanity. It is Moral Evil that we witnessed in Las Vegas in 2017 and in so many other murderous attacks on innocent people. The murder of millions and millions of people throughout history because they looked different or thought different or believe something different is Moral Evil. And I believe that the murder of millions of innocent defenseless unborn human beings is one of the greatest Moral Evils of our time.

There is also Supernatural Evil described in Revelation chapter 12. The prophet Daniel was also a witness of supernatural evil, Daniel 10:12-13: *"Then he said to me, "Do not fear, Daniel, for from the first day that you set your heart to understand, and to humble yourself before your God, your words were heard; and I have come because of your words. 13 But the prince of the kingdom of Persia withstood me twenty-one days; and behold, Michael, one of the chief princes, came to help me, for I had been left alone there with the kings of Persia."*

But out of evil comes what? Heroes! Through all the carnage that Sunday night in Las Vegas, we learned of incredible heroism. After the shots rang out and people began to fall, people, people of all colors and ethnicities, began to help each other. What is the second greatest commandment? **To love your neighbor as yourself**. Well you certainly can't love your neighbor more than to risk your life for them.

So, what is a Hero? One who shows great courage. Was King David a Hero? Yes, he was. He was a Hero to the nation of Israel when, as a teen he challenged Goliath to battle and using his AR-15 dropped him. Oh wait, I forgot, David used a sling and a rock to fell the toughest, biggest, fighting man in the Philistine army. David was a great and heroic leader for the nation of Israel. 1 Samuel 17:50: *"So David prevailed over the*

Philistine with a sling and a stone, and struck the Philistine and killed him. But there was no sword in the hand of David."

Ester was a hero for the Hebrew people. She did what she had to do, putting her life in danger to prevent the mass murder of the Hebrew people. Esther 4:10-13: *"Then Esther spoke to Hathach, and gave him a command for Mordecai: 11 "All the king's servants and the people of the king's provinces know that any man or woman who goes into the inner court to the king, who has not been called, he has but one law: put all to death, except the one to whom the king holds out the golden scepter, that he may live. Yet I myself have not been called to go in to the king these thirty days." 13 And Mordecai told them to answer Esther: "Do not think in your heart that you will escape in the king's palace any more than all the other Jews."*

Esther 5:1-2: *"Now it happened on the third day that Esther put on her royal robes and stood in the inner court of the king's palace, across from the king's house, while the king sat on his royal throne in the royal house, facing the entrance of the house. 2 So it was, when the king saw Queen Esther standing in the court, that she found favor in his sight, and the king held out to Esther the golden scepter that was in his hand. Then Esther went near and touched the top of the scepter."*

Without the actions of Esther, not only would Israel be destroyed, but the one person living at that time in the royal line of David that would lead to Jesus would have been killed as well.

Heroism was on full display that night in Las Vegas. There was this incredible picture of a woman on the ground with a man covering her with his body and I thought what a valiant thing to do, to protect his wife or girlfriend. Come to find out that the man was a young soldier and he didn't know the woman and yet he shielded her with his body until the immediate shooting stopped and then led her to safety.

Then there was Jonathan Smith who helped rescue and protect more than twenty people. While he was busy risking his life to save others, he was shot in the neck, but he survived. Jonathan was leading people away from the concert area into the parking lot getting them to hide behind the vehicles for protection. When he went to get several young women into better concealment, he was wounded in the neck. He was then saved by an off-duty police officer from San Diego who procured a ride to the hospital for Jonathan and stayed with him tending his wound.

That Sunday night in Las Vegas, Jack and Laurie Beaton were celebrating their 23rd wedding anniversary at the event. When the shooting began, she was nearly hit and her husband yelled for her to "get down, get down." When she did, Jack covered her with his body protecting her from the bullets. Laurie said that Jack told her that he loved her and then his body went limp. She was rescued by others and lost track of her beloved Jack. She would find out later that he had died protecting her. John 15:13; *"Greater love has no one than this, than to lay down one's life for his friends."*

This was true all through that terrible attack. Jesus said in John 15:12: *"This is My commandment, that you love one another as I have loved you."* And how much did Jesus love us? He died for us. Isn't it interesting that Christian or not, believer in the Bible or not, most human beings have an innate understanding of this commandment from Jesus? When things go bad as we have witnessed through the Las Vegas Shooting, the Covid-19 pandemic, and the civil unrest around the United States, many people fight their fear and move to help others in need. I posted this during the week following the Las Vegas shooting. It is not mine and it's called *"The Essence of a Hero."* "True heroism is remarkably sober, very undramatic. It is not the urge to surpass all others at whatever cost, but the urge to serve others whatever the cost" (Author unknown).

A Marine veteran from San Diego was at the concert in Las Vegas and he was able to escape by jumping over a fence with a friend. He then found a pick-up truck with the keys in it, took it and began transporting some of the more seriously wounded victims to the hospital. He was reportedly able to make two trips as the ambulances were just arriving on scene. Joshua 1:9: *"Have I not commanded you? Be strong and courageous. Do not be afraid; do not be discouraged, for the LORD your God will be with you wherever you go."*

There was also a couple there from Tennessee. When the shooting started, he placed himself as a shield for his wife and he was hit by the gunfire and died protecting her. The selfless acts of so many are absolutely amazing. Off-duty law enforcement officers, fire personal, and medical people were all just enjoying a concert one moment and in the next moment, they were rushing to protect others and help treat those hit by the hundreds of rounds fired into the crowd.

We have been witnessing this same type of heroic response to the Covid-19 pandemic by hospital workers, nurses, doctors, first responders and so many others. So many work-a-day people are now heroes to the nation; truckers, workers who keep the nation's food supply on track, grocery workers, food service workers and the list goes on. These are ordinary people who, like those who responded to help and protect during the Las Vegas shooting, were and are willing to assist their fellow human beings.

You know, there has been a lot of negativity thrown in the direction of law enforcement and admittedly some of it is deserved. What the world witnessed in Minneapolis, Minnesota on May 25, 2020 when George Floyd died while in police custody was a tragic and needless event. From that there have been calls for major Law Enforcement changes. Some of the proposed changes have probably been long overdue. But the bad is incredibly outweighed by the good like which we saw in Las Vegas that horrible Sunday night, as officers worked to save people and protect people from the murderous fire raining down on the crowd. They placed themselves in harm's way, they deliberately placed their patrol cars between the shooter and the victims making themselves the target not the people. Officers responded to the riots and did their best to protect the innocent people and property threatened by the rioters. Law enforcement and firefighters and other first responders worked continuously in the face of the Covid-19 pandemic. Some have died from this virus, but the protection of society continues to be their goal.

In the movie *13 Hours, the story of Benghazi*, after the battle is over and the folks are being evacuated, one lady looks at one of the shot-up operators and says,

"I don't know how you guys survived all that, but I know how the rest of us did."

That is true in many instances for those who survived the Las Vegas shooting and other violent attacks since then. Kaya Jones, is a singer and was in a bar after having performed before the final act when the Las Vegas shooting started. Inside the bar was another performer who had a concealed carry weapon who was approached by a law enforcement officer who was visiting the city and was not armed. At the time it was unknown if there were multiple shooters or whether they were on foot, so the officer asked the singer for the weapon so that he could guard the door and protect those inside.

A man in Chicago heard about the massacre and while he did not know anyone involved, he felt the need to craft 59 wooden crosses, painted white for those who had died. He then drove from Chicago to Las Vegas to set those crosses out in tribute to the fallen. That is a hero.

The men and women, husbands and wives, and fathers and mothers are heroes in the Covid-19 pandemic. They are having to respond to a vastly different way of living and surviving. So many things that were part of their regular routine just weeks before have now gone by the wayside. But their work to carry on with life is heroic. However, what acts of evil show us is that we truly need to be praying for God to send revival. Acts 4:27-31: *"For truly against Your holy Servant Jesus, whom You anointed, both Herod and Pontius Pilate, with the Gentiles and the people of Israel, were gathered together 28 to do whatever Your hand and Your purpose determined before to be done. 29 Now, Lord, look on their threats, and grant to Your servants that with all boldness they may speak Your word, 30 by stretching out Your hand to heal, and that signs and wonders may be done through the name of Your holy Servant Jesus." 31 And when they had prayed, the place where they were assembled together was shaken; and they were all filled with the Holy Spirit, and they spoke the word of God with boldness."*

We should be praying for the same thing, for God to send revival through the Holy Spirit, to strengthen us in order that we might stand against the moral, natural and supernatural evil that is roaming in our midst. 1 Peter 5:8: *"Be sober, be vigilant; because your adversary the devil walks about like a roaring lion, seeking whom he may devour. 9 Resist him, steadfast in the faith, knowing that the same sufferings are experienced by your brotherhood in the world."*

How can we resist? We can't unless we are filled with the power of God.

1 Peter 5:10-11: *"But may the God of all grace, who called us to His eternal glory by Christ Jesus, after you have suffered a while, perfect, establish, strengthen, and settle you. 11 To Him be the glory and the dominion forever and ever. Amen."*

4 Heroes, Kings, and Chess

Did you have one or more heroes when you were growing up? Maybe they were sports, or movie stars. Maybe they were just famous people. I'll bet you even have a hero or two today. But what is a hero?

Hero is defined as "somebody who is admired, somebody who commits an act of remarkable bravery, someone with courage and strength of character." Given those attributes, it is easy to see why it is so hard to find good heroes today. Oh, but we try don't we, we search for heroes in sports, the movies, on television, but somehow these would be heroes turn out to be human and fail us.

On a trip to Hungary some years ago, my wife and I arrived the day before the national recognition of Hungary's greatest hero, King Saint Stephen. August 20th in Hungary is like July 4th in the United States. On our first day in Hungary, we, along with a very dear friend walked around the town and visited some of the sites including Heroes Square. A great deal of Hungarian history is displayed in the construction and statues of this location.

As I was standing there in the midst of Hero's Square, knowing the history as I have learned, I watched as many people children, young people and adults climbed on some of the statues with no apparent understanding or realization of what this area really stood for. It was then that I felt a little, and I mean a very little about what the Apostle Paul maybe felt while standing on the Areopagus in Greece. In ancient Greece, the Greeks had an altar for every god they knew of, and just to make sure that their bases were covered, they even had an altar to the unknown god.

One major figure is the over 100-foot-tall Corinthian column which dominates the square. On top is the Archangel Gabriel who is holding St. Stephen's Crown. According to the story, Gabriel appeared to St. Stephen in his dream and offered him the crown of Hungary. Pope Sylvester II did send a crown acknowledging Hungary and King Stephen as a defender of Christendom. Today you can view the Holy Crown in the Hungarian Parliament building in Budapest.

The crown itself is a great testament to Christ. The upper part of the Holy Crown is the older one which was sent by Pope Sylvester II to Saint Stephen I, who became king and founded Hungary in 1000 A.D. in recognition of his mission to turn the pagan Hungarians to Christianity and to recognize the Hungarian state. It was joined to a lower part that today makes up the whole crown. On the top of the corona latina, an enameled golden plate shows Christ raising His right hand for blessing and holding a book in his left. The crossing metal straps of the top of the crown carries pictures of 8 Apostles. Ahead of Christ comes the picture of John and Bartholomew, to the right Peter and Andrew, to the left Paul and Philip, to the back James and Thomas. On the top plate of the arch a golden cross is mounted, which is not the original one. It is believed that the original cross was a relic holder and contained a little piece of the cross on which Christ was crucified. This cross was broken off and later replaced by the present one which was originally in an upright position. Its leaning posture is likely due to physical damage. The earliest representation of the Holy Crown dating from the 17th century already shows it in leaning position. The two parts, the lower circular Greek crown and the upper arch-type Latin crown was attached together by Hungarian King Geza I at the end of the 11th century, and it is proven that the complete Hungarian Holy Crown already existed in 1166. So, it is more than 800 years old.

Hungary was founded in 1000 A.D. by King Saint Stephen. He not only pulled the different tribes of peoples together to create a nation, but he was a Christian and determined that Hungary would be a Christian nation.

On April 4, 2010, over 1,300 people, all of them members of Faith Church in Budapest celebrated Resurrection Sunday in Budapest, Hungary. The video of the event held in Heroes Square went viral almost from the moment it was put on You Tube. In fact, you can google

Resurrection Dance 2010 and watch the video, it only takes about six minutes.

Here in the United States, many people say that we were not founded as a Christian nation. They refuse to look at the historical facts in the writings of the founding fathers as to their original intent. The same is true of Hungary, however their Christian heritage is on display. It is the Holy, Royal crown.

Standing there in Heroes Square, I realized that a large number of Hungarians, and even Hungary as a nation has forgotten their Christian roots. Sure, they have a holiday and many statues and buildings that show the original intent to be a Christian nation, but over time, like here in the United States, in England and many other parts of the world, Christianity and Jesus Christ have been reduced to story and legend or pushed out of the public conscience totally. I felt as I was standing there that the people, like the ancient Greeks, needed to know the truth about the unknown God that their history speaks of.

Let's look at Acts 17: 22-31: *"Then Paul stood in the midst of the Areopagus and said, "Men of Athens, I perceive that in all things you are very religious; 23 for as I was passing through and considering the objects of your worship, I even found an altar with this inscription: TO THE UNKNOWN GOD. Therefore, the One whom you worship without knowing, Him I proclaim to you: 24 God, who made the world and everything in it, since He is Lord of heaven and earth, does not dwell in temples made with hands. 25 Nor is He worshiped with men's hands, as though He needed anything, since He gives to all life, breath, and all things. 26 And He has made from one blood every nation of men to dwell on all the face of the earth, and has determined their preappointed times and the boundaries of their dwellings, 27 so that they should seek the Lord, in the hope that they might grope for Him and find Him, though He is not far from each one of us; 28 for in Him we live and move and have our being, as also some of your own poets have said, 'For we are also His offspring.' 29 Therefore, since we are the offspring of God, we ought not to think that the Divine Nature is like gold or silver or stone, something shaped by art and man's devising. 30 Truly, these times of ignorance God overlooked, but now commands all men everywhere to repent, 31 because He has appointed a day on which He will judge the world in righteousness by the Man whom He has ordained. He has given assurance of this to all by raising Him from the dead."*

So, what is Paul doing? He is informing the intellectuals of the time in Greece that this God can not only be known, but that He is the God above all other gods. He is the Creator God; He is the God of Salvation. I wonder if it had been written at the time, if Paul might have also cited John 1:1 through 3 to the Greeks: *"In the beginning was the Word, and the Word was with God, and the Word was God. 2 He was in the beginning with God. 3 All things were made through Him, and without Him nothing was made that was made."*

As I mentioned August 20th is the celebration of the founding of the nation of Hungary. It is also called the "Feast Day of Saint Stephen" or "Day of New Bread" representing the annual harvesting of wheat throughout Hungary. But to get Biblical, Jesus is called what? "The bread of life." And doesn't that just fit with the Hungarian celebration of new bread. Jesus is the new bread of eternal life. This day of celebration is so full of Christ and Christianity that if the Hungarians really recognized what was going on, they would be on their knees before Christ.

According to the New American Commentary, "The sermon in Acts 17 can be divided into five sections. Verses 22–23 introduce the main theme—the ignorance of the pagan worship. Verses 24–25 present the true object of worship, the Creator God, and the folly of idolatrous worship with temples and sacrifices. Verses 26–27 deal with the true relationship of human beings to their Creator, which is the central theme of Paul's message. Verse 28 provides a transition, capping off the argument of the relationship of persons to God and providing the basis for a renewed attack on idolatry in verse 29. The final two verses return to the original theme. The time of ignorance was now over. With revelation came a call to repent in light of the coming judgment and the resurrection of Christ."

The song from Resurrection Sunday has a rap section that covers the same basic thought:

When something in you, says you're not through, something whispers, you need to go too.

You say that things just can't stay this way, your heart is calling may day, may day,

world is just trouble, get out of your muddle, jump, now's the time, take your chance on the double.

Leave it behind, you'll see you won't mind, once you meet Jesus the answer you'll find

Don't google your noodle, or consult your poodle, just follow your heart and it will be super

Wake up, see the light, find new life in His life, with Him in sight He'll take you to new heights

The rescues begun, now Someone's come, be looking to the sky but not for Air Force One.

The way out is up; up up and away, with Jesus today is Independence Day

Paul in Greece was telling the Greeks that while they had a lot of heroes, small h, he wanted to share with them knowledge of the real Hero, capital H.

Remember the definition of a Hero? Somebody who is admired, somebody who commits an act of remarkable bravery, someone with courage and strength of character.

Have you ever heard the story about a chess master who saw a painting titled "Check Mate"? The painting depicted a chess match between a young man and Satan. It also showed that Satan was one move away from capturing the young man's King and winning the match and the young man's soul. The chess master as the story goes, set up the pieces on a chess board as they were in the painting and discovered that the young man's king still had one more move. Our King not only has one more move, He has the final move, the eternal checkmate of Satan and evil.

I want to talk some more about the King. The Old Testament Prophet Micah predicts the coming of the King in chapter 5 verse 2: *"Bethlehem Ephrathah, you are small among the clans of Judah; One will come from you to be ruler over Israel for Me. His origin is from antiquity, from eternity."*

In Genesis 1:1: we read: *"In the beginning God created the heavens and the earth."*

Creation was the first move in what would become the cosmic chess match that is currently going on between God and Satan.

Being the lead angel of God's angel corps wasn't enough for Lucifer, so he led a revolt against God. Satan and the Angels that followed him were cast out of heaven and down to earth. Satan wasted little time in his next move, as he convinced Eve that God was probably hiding the fact that she and Adam could also become like God if they ate of the forbidden fruit. Genesis 3:1- 5: *"Now the serpent was more cunning than any beast of the field which the LORD God had made. And he said to the woman, "Has God indeed said, 'You shall not eat of every tree of the garden'?" 2 And the woman said to the serpent, "We may eat the fruit of the trees of the garden; 3 but of the fruit of the tree which is in the midst of the garden, God has said, 'You shall not eat it, nor shall you touch it, lest you die.' " 4 Then the serpent said to the woman, "You will not surely die. 5 For God knows that in the day you eat of it your eyes will be opened, and you will be like God, knowing good and evil."*

Satan's next move was getting Cain to kill Able to cut of the Godly line. But God responded with the birth of Seth which restored the Godly line. Satan followed that by causing increasing wickedness in the world, to which God found a man named Noah, and as Dr. Tony Evans says, "God gave Noah a three word sermon "It's gonna rain" and God destroyed the world as the fountains of the deep broke up and the windows of heaven were opened.

Satan was not finished and he found a man called Nimrod, which means "let us rebel" and did he ever. Nimrod started to build the tower of Babel and very slyly began to distort God's Word into what is today astrology. But God responded by finding Abraham in Ur of the Chaldees, telling him to leave that country and that He, God, would make through Abraham a great nation.

This pattern of move, counter move continues throughout the Old Testament.

Then in the New Testament, God decides to move the King into the game by coming to earth as Jesus Christ and dying for the sins of all who would believe in Him. However, Satan was not finished. Knowing that he could not and cannot defeat God, Satan has decided to take as many pieces (humanity) from the cosmic game board as he can.

After Jesus is crucified and rises after the third day, Satan moves to create persecution for the new Christians. As they fan out from Jerusalem, God leads them to spread the word about Jesus and His saving grace. Then, about 64

A.D. plus or minus a few years, the Roman ruler Nero decides that Christianity is the reason for Rome's problems, so he begins a great persecution of Christians.

Some two hundred years later, Emperor Constantine says the God of the Christians is his God and mandates Christianity as the faith of the Roman Empire. Satan then moves by leading the Roman Catholic Church away from God and closer to the depravity of man. Some six hundred years later, the Catholic Church becomes very political, one of the main ways is by selling indulgences. That means that it was possible to pay the church for the sins you were going to commit and be forgiven in advance.

God's next move was the reformation that spread across Europe and the British Isles. The movement back toward God and the true teaching of the Bible was led by people like Martin Luther, John Smyth, Thomas Helways, and Huldrych Zwingli, among others. God used a variety of men to accomplish the reformation and to show that the movement was indeed from and by God and not of man.

Satan then hits on one of the greatest ideas he ever had. Create a way for people to question God and His Word by making false science appear to clearly differ and contradict God's

Word about creation. Now almost from the beginning, there has been opposition to creation and the origins of man, but it really seemed to pick up speed as the reformation became successful in returning people to the Word of God. In fact, many of our founding fathers were aware of the creation question and its importance.

Why is creation so important? Because Satan desires to undermine God's expressed account of creation. By denying creation it is easier to deny God's plan of salvation and the truth of all God's Word. If God is subtly removed from people's minds as their creator, then it is easier for them to disregard Him as their redeemer. Evolution and millions of years is Satan's effort to make you think that you are just some cosmic dust mixed with a little rain and amino acids. You are nothing special, you just happened to be at the top of the evolutionary ladder. Satan knows that if he can make people believe that we just happened," then we will forget or not believe that we are created in the image of God.

Chuck Norris in an article entitled "America's founding creationists" quotes a few of our founding fathers regarding the importance of this question. Thomas Pain said, "it has been the error of schools to teach astronomy and all the other sciences and subjects of natural philosophy, as accomplishments only; whereas they should be taught theologically, or with reference to the Being who is the Author of them: for all the principles of science are of divine origin. Man cannot make, or invent, or contrive principles; he can only discover them, and he ought to look through the discovery to the Author".

John Adams said, "It has long been-very long- a settled opinion in my mind that there is now, never will be, and never was but one Being who can understand the universe, and that it is not only vain but wicked for insects like us to pretend to comprehend it."

But Satan kicked the battle up a notch in the early 1800s when a young lawyer named Charles Lyell who was no fan of Christianity, published his first of three volumes of *Principles of Geology*. His main claim to fame was the development of the Geologic column. According to Lyell this column and subsequently the world of evolution, is that the layers of the earth are specific ages of the earth representing millions and millions of years of Earth's evolution and development. The only problem is that the Geologic column only exists in text books, because nowhere in the world are Lyell's proposed geologic layers to be found together.

It was Lyell's work that helped Charles Darwin's mind to come up with his book the *The Origin of Species.* These two men did a great deal to destroy people's faith and belief in God's Word.

Remember, Satan knows that the game is lost, he just wants to remove as many pieces (humanity) from the game board as possible. But why would God allow this to happen to something that He originally said was very good after He created us.

Do you know how God created? He spoke it out. He spoke to the darkness and light came out. He spoke to the water and fish and swimming creatures were created. He spoke to the earth and plants and animals came forth. In all things, God spoke to the source to create. Then, God said, *"let us make man in Our image,"* (Genesis 1:26) God spoke to the source and we were created in the image of God.

We are chosen., as the Apostle Paul writes in Ephesians chapter 1 verse 4: *"According as he hath chosen us in him before the foundation of the world,"*

Do you realize, that you and I and all humanity, are as Bishop Kenneth Ulmer says, *"are designed by the divine mind of God."* Yet Satan does not want you to believe that we are chosen by God even before the foundation of the world, so Satan developed evolution.

But I am sure that you might have asked why God would place His divine design out in public as it were for Satan to corrupt. I know that I used to. Then God gave me this thought. Many years ago, when my wife's mother passed away, she went back to help her brother sort things out. In her mother's closet she discovered several dozen collector plates, you know the special collector plates that depict different scenes and are designed to gain in value. Her mother had hidden them away in their Styrofoam boxes so that they would not be broken or damaged. And while the plates were not broken or damaged, they were never seen, their beauty and artistry were never displayed to anyone. When my wife brought them home, she decided that she would put them on display all over the house. We have scenes from the *Wizard of Oz*, *Gone with the Wind*, and many other beautiful depictions. But over the years, a few of the plates have been damaged or destroyed by accidents. Now you might say, "what a loss," and you would be right. But is it better to have had them on display for even a short time to bring beauty to our home for others to see or would it have been better to keep them hidden away?

Well for my wife, the choice was easy. She wanted to share these beautiful designs and pictures. And so does God with His divine design. Because God gave us free will, there has been from the beginning the chance that we would be broken or damaged. Yet God was so sure that His divine design would triumph, that He was and is willing to place us, you and me, whom He has chosen, on the cosmic chess board. God feels so good about us, that He is willing to set us before the evil of the universe, because He has chosen us for glory, He has chosen us for eternity, He has chosen us for an intimate relationship with Him. God has chosen me and you for Glory!

In Ephesians chapter 1 verses 11 through 14, we read: *"In Him also we have obtained an inheritance, being predestined according to the purpose of Him who works all things according to the counsel of His will, 12 that we who first trusted in Christ should be to the praise of His glory. 13 In Him you also trusted, after you heard the word of truth, the gospel of your salvation; in whom also, having believed, you were sealed with the Holy Spirit of promise, 14 who is the guarantee of our inheritance until the redemption of the purchased possession, to the praise of His glory."*

Here are three final thoughts as we draw this chapter to a close.

First: Adam and Eve were evicted from the Garden of Eden because they sinned against God. Satan was able to fool Eve because she did not have the same relationship with God that Adam had and Adam chose to disobey God. Remember, Adam walked with God, talked with God, and personally knew God. And that is our defense against Satan, having a strong walk with God, praying every day or talking with God, and studying the Word of God to have a strong personal knowledge of God.

Second: Satan is very resilient. He has the ability to reinvent himself for every age. However, his game is always the same and that is to get us to dis-believe in God and His Word. Currently the game is evolution and millions of years. But we can overcome this Satanic challenge by learning more about God's word. There are a great many resources concerning the fallacy of millions of years and bursting forth from nothing and evolving from a rock.

Finally: As God's divine design, we are put here on the Earth to reflect the image of God and His goodness. Remember, we were chosen before the foundation of the earth was laid. God went to the source, Himself when He spoke us out. He didn't consult another source, He didn't need a list to choose from, God spoke to Himself and created us in His image. Remember, we are chosen for glory, we are chosen as Christians to shine forth God's glory to all the earth so that we can help to save others for when His Son Jesus Christ returns to the earth and God can once again look at His creation and say that He is well pleased.

5 Surrounded by the Enemy

On June 25, 1876 there was a big battle that occurred. You might have heard about it. It was the Battle of Little Big Horn. You might know the story better as Custer's Last Stand.

On that morning, Lieutenant Colonel George A. Custer and the 7th Cavalry charged into battle against the Lakota Sioux and Northern Cheyenne Indians. Custer had orders to wait for reinforcements at the mouth of the Little Big Horn River before attacking the Indians, but Chief Sitting Bull had been spotted nearby, and Custer was impatient to attack.

A treaty had given the Sioux exclusive rights to the Black Hills, but when gold was later discovered in the area, white miners flocked to the territory. Despite the treaty, the U.S. government ordered the Indians away from the invading settlers and back to their reservations. Custer's job was to force the Indians back to their reservations. Some of the Indians refused to leave their sacred land, and other hunters were camped in remote places and never learned of the order. The U.S. Army prepared for battle.

Custer planned to attack the Indian camp from three sides, but Chief Sitting Bull was ready for them. The first two groups, led by Captain Benteen and Major Reno, were immediately forced to retreat to one side of the river, where they continued to fight as best they could. Custer was not as lucky.

Custer's troops charged the Indians from the north. Quickly encircled by their enemy, Custer and 265 of his soldiers were killed in less than an hour. The Indians retreated two days later when the troops Custer had been ordered to wait for arrived.

Have you seen the movie *Hacksaw Ridge*? It is the story of Desmond Doss, an Infantry Medic who was the first of only two Conscientious Objectors to ever be awarded the Congressional Medal of Honor. The second awardee was Thomas W. Bennett, a corporal who was also a combat medic in Vietnam and was killed in action attempting to rescue a fallen soldier. Doss was awarded the medal for his actions on the island of Okinawa from April 29 to May 21, 1945. During that time he found himself in the midst of the enemy several times while working to save and rescue fellow soldiers that had been wounded. Doss said in an interview that he asked God to help him save one more and after that Doss would ask the Lord to help him save one more, and continued asking.

King David experienced a similar feeling, that of being surrounded by his enemies.

Psalms 3: *"Lord, how they have increased who trouble me! Many are they who rise up against me. 2 Many are they who say of me, "There is no help for him in God." Selah 3 But You, O Lord, are a shield for me, My glory and the One who lifts up my head. 4 I cried to the Lord with my voice, And He heard me from His holy hill. Selah 5 I lay down and slept; I awoke, for the Lord sustained me. 6 I will not be afraid of ten thousands of people Who have set themselves against me all around. 7 Arise, O Lord; Save me, O my God! For You have struck all my enemies on the cheekbone; You have broken the teeth of the ungodly. 8 Salvation belongs to the Lord. Your blessing is upon Your people. Selah"*

What is going on that King David feels the need to write this to the Lord? He is the King! Well, David is fleeing from his son Absalom who is attempting an armed coup against his father. The whole story is in 2 Samuel chapters 15 through 18. Absalom and David didn't have the best Father Son relationship. In fact, they didn't have any relationship at all. Absalom was so angry with his father the King that he determined to remove his father from the throne. 2 Samuel 15:10; *"Then Absalom sent spies throughout all the tribes of Israel, saying, "As soon as you hear the sound of the trumpet, then you shall say, 'Absalom reigns in Hebron!'"*

I bet I am not the only one who has had someone plan evil against them for whatever reason. And when the attack comes, it can feel sometimes like we are surrounded by attackers. Satan can rile up people and events that make it seem like we are part of Custer's 7th Cavalry at the Little Big Horn, feeling that there is no way out! What can we do?

Look at what King David writes at the beginning of Psalm 3: *"Lord, how they have increased who trouble me! Many are they who rise up against me."* David begins with what? Lord! Sometimes you need to get right to the point, particularly if you feel that you don't have much time. So many of us at some time in our life have probably felt this way and with the Covid-19 pandemic, or with all the civil unrest, so many people feel and have felt they were surrounded by the enemy. What enemy you might ask? Sickness, death of a loved one or friend, loss of your job and income, feeling depressed and like there will be no end. It is so easy to feel surrounded by negativity when it seems to be all we see, hear, and read. Remember when the

Apostle Peter walked on the water? Matthew 14:30: *"But when he saw that the wind was boisterous, he was afraid; and beginning to sink he cried out, saying, "Lord, save me!"* Peter saw that his surroundings were difficult, his faith faded, and he cried for help.

King David's son Absalom had over time built up a following and then turned in open rebellion against his father. Why was this happening? David was living what the prophet Nathan had told him. We read it here in 2 Samuel 12:10-15: *"Now therefore, the sword shall never depart from your house, because you have despised Me, and have taken the wife of Uriah the Hittite to be your wife.' 11 Thus says the Lord: 'Behold, I will raise up adversity against you from your own house; and I will take your wives before your eyes and give them to your neighbor, and he shall lie with your wives in the sight of this sun. 12 For you did it secretly, but I will do this thing before all Israel, before the sun.'" 13 So David said to Nathan, "I have sinned against the Lord." And Nathan said to David, "The Lord also has put away your sin; you shall not die. 14 However, because by this deed you have given great occasion to the enemies of the Lord to blaspheme, the child also who is born to you shall surely die." 15 Then Nathan departed to his house."*

David cries out; "Lord, look at how many have turned against me, many are rising up in rebellion." What does it feel like when people we know, or our supposed friends, rise up against us? Well there may not be an intended result of our being killed, but the feeling can be scary and terrifying anyway. It seems that more and more if a person has a different viewpoint from others they are attacked on Social Media and verbally in person. We have apparently lost the art of conversation and go straight to the argument. Many times we cannot even agree to disagree without animosity toward the other person. What can we do when these feelings threaten to wash over us like a tsunami? Just what David and Peter did, cry out to the Lord to save you.

Look at verse 2; *Many are they who say of me, "There is no help for him in God."* King David laments here that people are saying that God will not help him in his time of need. Have you ever felt like that? Satan is always happy in tense situations to inform you that God will not help you this time, God will not comfort or guide you this time because you have stepped over the line once too often.

I have felt this, and it can be crushing spiritually until you see through the spiritual haze and remember that God is a forgiving God and always stands ready to help.

And this fact is what David is saying in verse 3: *"But You, O Lord, are a shield for me, My glory and the One who lifts up my head."* David you need to remember was not a weak person. He was a warrior, a fighter who understood the power and strength of God. God loves to be our shield against adversity, evil and all the "travails" in our life. A shield is designed to protect a person from blows against them; that is what God does as our shield. Genesis 15:1: *"After these things the word of the Lord came to Abram in a vision, saying, "Do not be afraid, Abram. I am your shield, your exceedingly great reward."* The Apostle Paul understood this as he wrote in Romans 8:3: *"What then shall we say to these things? If God is for us, who can be against us?"*

Benjamin Franklin, a believer in God as a protector, said this as Governor of Pennsylvania in 1778 as he proclaimed the State's first day of fasting; "It is the duty of mankind on all suitable occasions to acknowledge their dependence on the divine being...that Almighty God would mercifully interpose and still the rage of war among the nations...and that He would take this province under His protection, confound the designs and defeat the attempts of its enemies, and unite our hearts and strengthen our hands in every undertaking that may be for the public good, and for our defense and security in this time of danger."

What is Benjamin Franklin asking of the Lord? To be a shield, to protect the people of Pennsylvania and America. People who know the Lord cry out because they know that He will hear them, just as David knew this in verse 4: *"I cried to the Lord with my voice, And He heard me from His holy hill."* Why would David believe this? Maybe because he had some past experiences with God hearing and answering his prayers. Absalom had attacked with the intent of killing a King specifically chosen by God. When you attack what God chooses that is usually not a good idea. And remember what the prophet Nathan told David, that God said David would not be killed.

However, during this attack, all David had on his mind was surviving. To do that he needed to cry out to God. What happens next? Let's look at verses 5 and 6.

"I lay down and slept; I awoke, for the Lord sustained me. 6 I will not be afraid of ten thousands of people Who have set themselves against me all around." David knew that his belief and faith in God's protection was real and that enabled him to go to sleep.

The Apostle Peter and the other Apostles were scared and frightened during a storm, but they learned that they could lean on the Lord. Matthew 8:23-27: *" Now when He got into a boat, His disciples followed Him. 24 And suddenly a great tempest arose on the sea, so that the boat was covered with the waves. But He was asleep. 25 Then His disciples came to Him and awoke Him, saying, "Lord, save us! We are perishing!" 26 But He said to them, "Why are you fearful, O you of little faith?" Then He arose and rebuked the winds and the sea, and there was a great calm. 27 So the men marveled, saying, "Who can this be, that even the winds and the sea obey Him?"* Why was Jesus able to sleep? Because He knew that tragedy would not overtake them. But the Apostles' faith was not what it should have been for which Jesus admonished them. But what did they cry out? "Lord save us." David did the same thing, and he had complete faith that the Lord would protect and save him.

I'm sure there have been times that you like myself have cried out "Lord save me." In times of personal crisis, when we are pushed up against that emotional and spiritual wall and there is no apparent way out, we can and should cry out "Lord save me." The whole nation of Israel seemed to want David's head on a stick, but because he had faith in God as his shield, he could literally lay down and get a good night's sleep. Why? Oliver Cromwell, the Lord High Protector of England in the 1600's is quoted as saying this, "I have learned that if you fear God, you have no one else to fear." Well, David certainly feared the Lord and the Lord proved that David had nothing to fear from men.

This is the belief that we should have today regarding the various attacks that are being perpetrated against our current administration, but more importantly, against Christianity here in the United States. Satan has opened an all-out attack against Christianity here in the U.S. and many people are afraid or cowed by the anti-Christian onslaught. Look at what we witnessed during the Covid-19 crisis as many elected leaders ordered Christian churches to totally close, even when those congregations assembled in the church parking lot, stayed in their cars and listened to the Pastor's message via the radio. Church members were cited for illegally gathering.

Just a little Constitutional recollection of Amendment I

Congress shall make no law respecting an establishment of religion, or prohibiting the free exercise thereof; or abridging the freedom of speech, or of the press; or the right of the people peaceably to assemble, and to petition the government for a redress of grievances.

\Additionally, there is Supremacy Clause ARTICLE VI, CLAUSE 2; *This Constitution, and the Laws of the United States which shall be made in Pursuance thereof; and all Treaties made, or which shall be made, under the Authority of the United States, shall be the supreme Law of the Land; and the Judges in every State shall be bound thereby, any Thing in the Constitution or Laws of any State to the Contrary notwithstanding.*

This is part of the statement on April 14, 2020 by United States Attorney General William Barr:

"To contain the virus and protect the most vulnerable among us, Americans have been asked, for a limited period of time, to practice rigorous social distancing. The President has also asked Americans to listen to and follow directions issued by state and local authorities regarding social distancing. Social distancing, while difficult and unfamiliar for a nation that has long prided itself on the strength of its voluntary associations, has the potential to save hundreds of thousands of American lives from an imminent threat. Scrupulously observing these guidelines is the best path to swiftly ending COVID-19's

profound disruptions to our national life and resuming the normal economic life of our country. Citizens who seek to do otherwise are not merely assuming risk with respect to themselves, but are exposing others to danger. In exigent circumstances, when the community as a whole faces an impending harm of this magnitude, and where the measures are tailored to meeting the imminent danger, the constitution does allow some temporary restriction on our liberties that would not be tolerated in normal circumstances.

But even in times of emergency, when reasonable and temporary restrictions are placed on rights, the First Amendment and federal statutory law prohibit discrimination against religious institutions and religious believers. Thus, government may not impose special restrictions on religious activity that do not also apply to similar nonreligious activity. For example, if a government allows movie theaters, restaurants, concert halls, and other comparable places of assembly to remain open and unrestricted, it may not order houses of worship to close, limit their congregation size, or otherwise impede religious gatherings. Religious institutions must not be singled out for special burdens."

I believe that we need to be following the advice of Cromwell, *"I have learned that if you fear God, you have no one else to fear."* We need to pray for God's shield in our life, the life of our church, our nation, and for the world. Because when you do call on God to be your shield, look what happens. Let's read verses 7 and 8 from Psalm 3 again, *"Arise, O Lord; Save me, O my God! For You have struck all my enemies on the cheekbone; You have broken the teeth of the ungodly. 8 Salvation belongs to the Lord. Your blessing is upon Your people."*

David apparently awakes in a great mood because of the Lord. "Arise, O Lord." It seems that David is thanking God for what He had done and for what you are going to do seems to be what David is saying.

God is ready and willing to strike your enemies on the "cheekbones" in protection of you. We need to have the courage, belief, and faith to call on the Lord in the fashion that David, Peter, and others have. Our faith is under attack, and our God is under attack, but we know the same thing that David knew, and that is God is our shield and that God will have the ultimate triumph. Ephesians 6:16: *"above all, taking the shield of faith with which you will be able to quench all the fiery darts of the wicked one."* In the days of Paul and the Roman Empire, a Roman soldier's shield was about 2 and a half feet wide and four feet long. Pretty good protection. It was overlaid with linen and leather in order to allow it to absorb the fiery arrows of the enemy. With our faith in God standing before us, we can absorb the attack of Satan against us. Is Jesus Christ your shield?

6 Red Sky Warning

Back in 1998, Dr. Bill Bright, co-founder of Campus Crusade for Christ International along with Author John Damoose wrote a book titled *"Red Sky in the Morning."* The purpose of the book was to pose a question to Christians in America, "What Would Jesus Do about the moral and spiritual decline in America today?" How much more does that question need to be asked now and an answer found.

You might have recognized the title of the book as being based on an old Sailor's rhyme, "Red sky in the morning, sailor take warning.

Red sky at night, sailor's delight."

This is from the opening of chapter one; "As society enters the third millennium since the birth of Christ, we find America in the midst of a grave internal crisis that poses a threat to our existence. A "red sky" is rising in our nation, warning all who read the signs that we are indeed on the verge of moral and spiritual collapse." This was written in 1998, twenty-one years ago.

since 2000, the morals and ethics of society have been declining and breaking down at a breakneck pace. The standard today seems to be that there is no standard and if a person seeks to express or impose a standard, you are some type of bigot, racial, sexual, gender, whatever.

More and more today, people are throwing off standards and morals. In a 2014 study regarding the acceptance of homosexuality by the Williams Institute, participants were asked about their views on "Sexual relations between two adults of the same sex." In the United States in 1991, 67.4% said it was always wrong. In 2008, those who selected "always wrong" was down to 53.6%. Today that number is even lower.

The spirituality in the United States has also been on a downward slide. This is not a new thought. President Abraham Lincoln spoke of this in regard to what might be the downfall of the United States. This is from his January 27, 1838 speech to the Young Men's Lyceum of Springfield, Illinois:

"In the great journal of things happening under the sun, we, the American People, find our account running, under date of the nineteenth century of the Christian era.--We find ourselves in the peaceful possession, of the fairest portion of the earth, as regards extent of territory, fertility of soil, and salubrity of climate. We find ourselves under the government of a system of political institutions, conducing more essentially to the ends of civil and religious liberty, than any of which the history of former times tells us. We, when

80

mounting the stage of existence, found ourselves the legal inheritors of these fundamental blessings. We toiled not in the acquirement or establishment of them--they are a legacy bequeathed us, by a once hardy, brave, and patriotic but now lamented and departed race of ancestors. Their's was the task (and nobly they performed it) to possess themselves, and through themselves, us, of this goodly land; and to uprear upon its hills and its valleys, a political edifice of liberty and equal rights; 'tis ours only, to transmit these, the former, unprofaned by the foot of an invader; the latter, undecayed by the lapse of time and untorn by usurpation, to the latest generation that fate shall permit the world to know. This task of gratitude to our fathers, justice to ourselves, duty to posterity, and love for our species in general, all imperatively require us faithfully to perform.

How then shall we perform it?--At what point shall we expect the approach of danger? By what means shall we fortify against it?-- Shall we expect some transatlantic military giant, to step the Ocean, and crush us at a blow? Never! All the armies of Europe, Asia and Africa combined, with all the treasure of the earth (our own excepted) in their military chest; with a Bonaparte for a commander, could not by force, take a drink from the Ohio, or make a track on the Blue Ridge, in a trial of a thousand years.

At what point then is the approach of danger to be expected? I answer, if it ever reaches us, it must spring up amongst us. It cannot come from abroad. If destruction be our lot, we must ourselves be its author and finisher. As a nation of freemen, we must live through all time, or die by suicide.

I hope I am over wary; but if I am not, there is, even now, something of ill-omen, amongst us. *I mean the increasing disregard for law which pervades the country; the growing disposition to substitute the wild and furious passions, in lieu of the sober judgment of Courts; and the worse than savage mobs, for the executive ministers of justice. This disposition is awfully fearful in any community; and that it now exists in ours, though grating to our feelings to admit, it would be a violation of truth, and an insult to our intelligence, to deny."*

This is so very true today isn't it? We have been witnessing mob rule, and this has been true almost from the very beginning. As people have turned away from the Lord and toward their own counsel and ideas, society in all ways has declined_and, in some cases, resulted in the destruction of that society.

In the book of Amos chapters one and two, the Prophet Amos delivers God's judgment on the gentile nations that surrounded Israel and Judah. He shares God's judgment against Israel and Judah. Each judgment began with "for three transgressions and for four" and

Amos would lay out what these transgressions were.

Amos was telling the inhabitants of Judah that for three sins, their faithlessness is complete. The fourth sin is the final straw if you will, the tipping point, the point of no return regarding God's patience with Judah. So, what were Judah's sins against God according to the Prophet Amos? They had despised the law of the Lord and had not kept His commandments. Their lies led them astray. Lies which their fathers followed. Israel had agreed to follow, believe in and serve the God of Moses, the God of Abraham, Isaac, and Jacob, but as time went by, they were seduced by evil and began to turn away from all that God had warned them about.

Deuteronomy 8:19: *"Then it shall be, if you by any means forget the Lord your God, and follow other gods, and serve them and worship them, I testify against you this day that you shall surely perish."*

America fits this charge from Amos, in that America, for three transgressions and for four. Now I am not equating America and ancient Judah in that God may destroy us, not that we probably don't deserve it, but the ancient Jews were in violation of the Mosaic covenant that they had agreed to follow. God warned them for a few hundred years what would happen if they did not repent and return to Him, but they continued to rebel against

Is It Well With Your Soul?

God and He finally had enough and Israel was destroyed by the Assyrians. Later, Judah was destroyed by the Babylonians.

As I mentioned earlier, you can easily read God's condemnation of Judah, replace it with America and unfortunately it fits all too well. How, you might ask? Well let's look at America's sins. Because they have increasingly despised the law of the Lord, surveys show that fewer and fewer people believe in God. Additionally, 52% of people that say they believe in Jesus also believe that He sinned. If there is no belief in God, then we also see less belief in the Ten Commandments and basic right and wrong. The Apostle Paul spoke on this when he wrote to his young Pastoral friend Timothy,

2 Timothy 3:1-4: *"But know this, that in the last days perilous times will come: 2 For men will be lovers of themselves, lovers of money, boasters, proud, blasphemers, disobedient to parents, unthankful, unholy, 3 unloving, unforgiving, slanderers, without self-control, brutal, despisers of good, 4 traitors, headstrong, haughty, lovers of pleasure rather than lovers of God."*

Sound like anyone or anything you know today? This message from the Apostle Paul fits very well into the America of today doesn't it? What else does Amos accuse Judah of that fits America? "And have not kept His commandments." Virtually every

84

commandment of God is violated here in America. We place many other gods before the God of Creation, we don't love our neighbors for the most part, we murder millions of unborn defenseless babies on the altar of personal convenience, we covet the property of others and, if possible, we contrive a way to take it from them. We engage in slander against those we sometimes don't even know merely for not agreeing with us.

And finally, "their lies lead them astray, Lies which their fathers followed." Ken Ham, the president of Answers in Genesis has said many times regarding allowing wrong thinking and actions that are against the true meaning of Scripture into our lives, "I've said it many times before—when you open the door to compromise in Genesis, it doesn't take long for other doctrines to fall."

This shows us how accurate Dr. Bright's book *Red Sky in the Morning* was and is. In fact, this sailors warning that we read before; "Red sky in the morning, sailor take warning. Red sky at night, sailor's delight," was actually spoken first by Jesus while talking to the Pharisees in Matthew chapter 16 verses 1 through 3: *"Then the Pharisees and Sadducees came, and testing Him asked that He would show them a sign from heaven. 2 He answered and said to them, "When it is evening you say, 'It will be fair weather, for the sky is red'; 3 and in the morning, 'It will be foul weather today, for the sky is red and threatening.' Hypocrites! You know how to discern the face of the sky, but you cannot discern the signs of the times."*

As Christians we need to listen to this warning. We need to continue to move forward in the name of Jesus our Savior.

I would submit that the time for warning has passed and the time for dealing with the storm is upon us. We need to turn into the storm and stand our ground. How do we do that you might ask? Most importantly we must stand on Sola Scriptura, Scripture alone, as our foundation of belief and faith. We must throw aside the ideas of man, the created being, and grasp the ideas of the Creator.

Belief in the ideas of man is what we have been seeing really since the late 1700s and it has grown exponentially as we have moved into the 21st century. Evolution and millions of years have been the catalyst and driving force to undermine and destroy not only Scripture and God, but humanity itself. It is the belief in evolution that has created racism, and that has created the idea that some so-called races of humans are less advanced and less deserving of survival. The people who created the lies have been able to get people of different generations to believe the lies, and the children of those generations now believe and advance those lies.

A new study shows that 51% of professing evangelicals agree with the statement, "God accepts the worship of all religions, including Christianity, Judaism, and Islam." John 14:6: *"Jesus said to him, "I am the way, the truth, and the life. No one comes to the Father except through Me."* This statement by Jesus, the God of Creation, would seem to end any further thought about the many religions of belief. So, where does this come from? It comes from man and his reluctance to believe fully in the God of the Bible. It comes from man who steadfastly denies the exclusivity of the God of the Bible. It comes from man and his belief in science as more authoritative than Scripture.

"The 2018 State of Theology survey reveals deep confusion about the Bible's teaching, not only among Americans as a whole, but also among evangelicals. There is something very wrong when a majority of Americans can give the correct answers to basic Bible questions and at the same time say that their beliefs are purely a matter of personal opinion. These results show the urgent need for sound biblical teaching and the bold preaching of the gospel. Millions of people do not understand the holiness of God, the reality of sin, and the one way of salvation in Jesus Christ. There is much work to be done, but it is our hope that these findings will serve the church in its efforts to reach more people with the faithful proclamation of the truth of God's Word." (stateoftheology.com)

We as Christians are the only group of people on the earth that can be attacked with impunity. It apparently does not matter what the problem is, we are the scape goat. In 2018 the great surgeon Dr. Ben Carson was speaking to over four hundred attendees of the Young Black Leadership Summit, which is a gathering for young black conservatives. As he was closing, he told the attendees two very important thoughts. The first was "your goal needs to be to do what is right, not just what will make you popular." And isn't that so true? The second thought was, "don't let haters dictate who you are." And we sure see a lot of that, especially for Christians.

However, as Christians, we should not be surprised since we were warned by Jesus Himself, John 15:18-19: *"If the world hates you, you know that it hated Me before it hated you. 19 If you were of the world, the world would love its own. Yet because you are not of the world, but I chose you out of the world, therefore the world hates you."* We witness this almost every day, but we also need to remember that Jesus is the foundation that our spiritual houses are built on and that is the strongest foundation in the universe, Luke 6:46-49: *"But why do you call Me 'Lord, Lord,' and not do the things which I say? 47 Whoever comes to Me, and hears My sayings and does them, I will show you whom he is like: 48 He is like a man building a house, who dug deep and laid the foundation on the rock. And when the flood arose, the stream beat vehemently against that house, and could not shake it, for it was founded on the rock. 49 But he who heard and did nothing is like a man who built a house on the earth without a foundation, against which the stream beat vehemently; and immediately it fell. And the ruin of that house was great."*

I believe that part of the "Red Sky in the Morning" warning must be to learn and share more of the foundational truths of God, Jesus, and the Scripture. We must be able to talk knowledgably about what the Bible says. We also need to be sure that we are sharing this information with our children. Parents are tasked by God to teach our children about what Scripture says in the Old Testament, about Creation and the other events of human history, to show why Creation is the more logical beginning of mankind. We are to give our children the knowledge and ability to respond to the attacks of the world.

7 Are We Without Remedy?

What does "Remedy" mean? It can mean a medicine or treatment for a disease or injury, or it can mean to set right (an undesirable situation). It is this second meaning that I am interested in. However, the entire world has been forced to search for a remedy of the first kind because of the Covid-19 pandemic. On Easter Sunday during the pandemic I shared a message titled "The Resurrection is Our Remedy." This is some of what I said, "Well here we are online instead of meeting together. But you know what is not quarantined. the sun rising this morning just like it did on the day of Jesus' resurrection. Second is the rising of the Son of God who stepped forth from the tomb as a sign that death had been defeated. A sign to mankind that Jesus could and would provide eternal life.

And why do we need this Remedy, this Risen Son of God? Because of what we read in 2 Chronicles 36:15-16: "And the Lord God of their fathers sent warnings to them by His messengers, rising up early and sending them, because He had compassion on His people and on His dwelling place. 16 But they mocked the messengers of God, despised His words, and scoffed at His prophets, until the wrath of the

Lord arose against His people, till there was no remedy."

I am not saying that the Covid-19 pandemic is or was a punishment from God, however, it was very scary for a great many people around the world. From early on, governments around the world were searching for a remedy to this unknown virus that was contagious and proved to be fatal in certain instances. When I searched online the phrase "search for covid-19 remedy on April 20, 2020" I received 208-million hits on Google. There are or were some treatments or remedies that helped against the Covid-19 and its symptoms, but a vaccine was a long way off. Wouldn't it be great if we could find a 100% certain remedy to this virus? Wouldn't it be great if we could find a 100% remedy for all disease and sickness around the world? Well, I am afraid that that is not going to be the case until Jesus Christ returns to the earth.

I am sure that many of us or even most of us have or do know a person that has struggled with cancer and the person might have died from their cancer because there was no remedy. A very good friend of mine's wife died several years ago from cancer. She was in her early 40s and had recovered from cancer through a tough regimen of treatment only to have it return and be told that this time there was no treatment or remedy that could help. This was an extraordinarily strong and faithful Christian woman. In fact, she even completed a police academy while she was undergoing cancer treatments the first time after her diagnosis.

The last night of her life with her husband at her side, she helped to plan her memorial service. She was very definite that those who gathered must be told two things. The first was that she did not blame God for what had happened and that they should not blame Him either. Second was that an invitation for the saving grace of Jesus Christ would be given. I was there and both conditions were met.

Why was this important to her? Because even at death's door, she loved her Savior, Jesus Christ and wanted others to have the same opportunity or remedy for eternal life that she had.

You see, in the Old Testament you find that many of the Prophets were involved in sharing the warnings of God in response to the rebellion of Israel and Judah against God and His Laws. For more than two hundred years, Prophets came and went each sharing the similar message of God's anger at the Jewish people. In the book of Amos, the Prophet shares a series of messages about God's anger and accusations against the nations that surrounded Israel and Judah. And then when the Israelites thought that they were home free, God through Amos lowers the boom!

Amos 5:14-15: *"Seek good and not evil, That you may live; So the Lord God of hosts will be with you, As you have spoken. 15 Hate evil, love good; Establish justice in the gate. It may be that the Lord God of hosts Will be gracious to the remnant of Joseph." This is basically the overriding theme of the prophets in their God given messages to Israel and Judah; God will forgive but only to a point. Both Israel and later Judah decided to ignore the prophets and their message from God until* **till there was no remedy.**

Iniquity and evil are just as prevalent today as they were in ancient Biblical times.

As I shared in the preface, this is From Dr. Albert Mohler, President of The Southern Baptist Seminary's Daily Briefing on April 2nd, 2020 regarding New York's dislike of Samaritan's Purse's hospital that was set up in Central Park to assist the city with medical response; "In its own way, New York City wants the hospital, but it doesn't want the Christian ministry behind it. It desperately needs this field hospital, but it doesn't want the hospital being brought by Samaritan's Purse. But just consider this for a moment. It really doesn't have any choice. It turns out that in many cases, the only organizations able to help are those Christian organizations that are ready to help precisely because of an extension of their Christian mission. They want Christian doctors and nurses to come to New York City, but they only want the doctor and nurse part not the

Christian part. But no one seems to be asking the question, why are they going? Because the answer to that question is they're going precisely because they are Christians."

Genesis 6:5-8: *"Then the Lord saw that the wickedness of man was great in the earth, and that every intent of the thoughts of his heart was only evil continually. 6 And the Lord was sorry that He had made man on the earth, and He was grieved in His heart. 7 So the Lord said, "I will destroy man whom I have created from the face of the earth, both man and beast, creeping thing and birds of the air, for I am sorry that I have made them." 8 But Noah found grace in the eyes of the Lord."* But Noah found grace in the eyes of the Lord, here comes a remedy for the future of humanity. Why, because it would be through Noah and his family that God would provide a remedy for the survival of humanity.

But wait, what about the people of Noah's time? Well God is long suffering and patient, but when time's up, that's it. Genesis 7:4: *"For after seven more days I will cause it to rain on the earth forty days and forty nights, and I will destroy from the face of the earth all living things that I have made."* The people had over 100 years to get the message, but they refused. Yet our patient God waited seven more days for anyone who would repent and follow Him to get on the Ark. At that point the remedy was gone and nothing but what was on the Ark would survive.

During the time of the Prophets, Israel and Judah had approximately 230 years to repent and return to the Lord. God doesn't post the expiration date but He warns us and leaves the decisions up to humanity. He created us with free will and He is willing to allow us to exercise that free will even if it leads to our demise. But is that it? There has to be another way, a remedy! And there is and we see that in what God told the Jews in the book of Amos chapter 5 verse 4: *"For thus says the Lord to the house of Israel: 'Seek Me and live.'"* Seek God and live! That is also a call to humanity, seek God and live. Except that call today does not go through prophets, it goes through the Gospel, the good news, which is what Gospel means, the good news of the salvation provided through the death and resurrection of Jesus Christ.

C. H. Henry said this regarding why God shares with humanity at all "God's personal gift to humanity is that He forfeits His personal privacy so that His sinful creatures may know Him." God does not owe us anything, no favors, no gifts, no grace, no explanations. Yet he does these things because of His love for His creation.

America, oh America, what dark trails have you followed, what evils you have embraced. Once a glimmering land from sea to shining sea, you have become a killing field of unborn defenseless babes. America, oh America why have you turned away from the

Christian roots of your founding that led to an exceptional greatness, a leader for what was right and good. America, oh America, you have fallen into the depths of depravity, turning against all that God commands, you have mocked God, despised His Words, and scoffed at those who share His message. America, oh America, you have turned into Israel and Judah who scorned the Lord and reaped their sad reward.

Romans 1:18-32: *"For the wrath of God is revealed from heaven against all ungodliness and unrighteousness of men, who suppress the truth in unrighteousness, 19 because what may be known of God is manifest in them, for God has shown it to them. 20 For since the creation of the world His invisible attributes are clearly seen, being understood by the things that are made, even His eternal power and Godhead, so that they are without excuse, 21 because, although they knew God, they did not glorify Him as God, nor were thankful, but became futile in their thoughts, and their foolish hearts were darkened. 22 Professing to be wise, they became fools, 23 and changed the glory of the incorruptible God into an image made like corruptible man — and birds and four-footed animals and creeping things. 24 Therefore God also gave them up to uncleanness, in the lusts of their hearts, to dishonor their bodies among themselves, 25 who exchanged the truth of God for the lie, and worshiped and served the creature rather than the Creator, who is blessed forever. Amen.*

26 For this reason God gave them up to vile passions. For even their women exchanged the natural use for what is against nature. 27 Likewise also the men, leaving the natural use of the woman, burned in their lust for one another, men with men committing what is shameful, and receiving in themselves the penalty of their error which was due.

28 And even as they did not like to retain God in their knowledge, God gave them over to a debased mind, to do those things which are not fitting; 29 being filled with all unrighteousness, sexual immorality, wickedness, covetousness, maliciousness; full of envy, murder, strife, deceit, evil-mindedness; they are whisperers, 30 backbiters, haters of God, violent, proud, boasters, inventors of evil things, disobedient to parents, 31 undiscerning, untrustworthy, unloving, unforgiving, unmerciful; 32 who, knowing the righteous judgment of God, that those who practice such things are deserving of death, not only do the same but also approve of those who practice them."

Paul is telling us that mankind is in real trouble without the remedy. In the movie the Ten Commandments with Charlton Heston as Moses, there is a scene where the adoptive mother of Moses, an Egyptian princess named Bithia is telling Moses who just discovered that he is a Hebrew that "this desert God (the Hebrew God) is the hope of the hopeless." However, as we have seen from the beginning of Creation, mankind sinned and by that sin rejected God and entered the hopeless situation of eternal punishment. However, this God is the God of not only the hopeless, but the God of the hopeful as well.

From the moment when Adam and Eve disobeyed God and were separated from Him, He has been providing a way back to Him. Humanity has gone from no remedy to having "THE REMEDY!" God is a gracious, caring, and merciful God. But God is also a God of Law and Judgment! Many people do not want to recognize the Law and Judgment part of God. That is a mistake and that failure is how you wind up in the position of "till there is no remedy."

I don't know if you realize this, but God's remedies have a shelf life. In the days of Noah God says in Genesis 6:3: *"And the Lord said, "My Spirit shall not strive with man forever, for he is indeed flesh; yet his days shall be one hundred and twenty years."* As God reminded humanity here and later Israel and Judah and now, this warning also has meaning for the world today. As I mentioned before, God created us with free will and He is willing to allow us to exercise that freewill even if it leads to our demise.

God's REMEDY for the salvation of humanity wasn't the birth of Jesus, but the resurrection of Jesus Christ. By allowing Himself to be sacrificed on the cross and take upon Himself all the sins of humanity past, present, and future, Jesus paid the price. He became the propitiation for us, Jesus became sinful for us before His Father.

And what's more, we do not have an excuse. You've heard the old adage: ignorance of the law is no defense. All citizens are charged with knowing the law. Well where do you think modern man came up with that idea? Atheists and others who deny God still understand this important thought. Men know what is legal and illegal, what is right and wrong. WHY? Because God wrote it in our basic operating system.

That is why even people who have never heard of God or Jesus or the Ten Commandants know in their soul that there is right and wrong. They know that there is something greater than they are. That is why every people group worships some type of God. Even if they are deep in an African jungle, an island lost to the world, or the Australian outback, people worship some type of God.

For the law of man, some lawyers say, "Even though ignorance of the law is not a defense, your specific lack of intent can be a defense. In order to convict you of an offense, the state does not have to prove that you were aware of a specific law, but they are generally required to prove that you intended the conduct that resulted in the violation." (freelegaladvice.com). That advice might work for man's laws, but it is lousy advice for God's Law.

That is because as Paul says in Romans chapter 1 verse 20: *"For since the creation of the world His invisible attributes are clearly seen, being understood by the things that are made, even His eternal power and Godhead, so that they are without excuse,"* or **till there is no remedy.**

Why do you think it is that the Creation account is so vehemently and relentlessly attacked? Think about Genesis chapter 1: In the beginning God created And the Spirit of God was hovering over the face of the waters. Then God said, And God saw, Then God said, Thus God made, And God called, And God saw that it was good.

Genesis chapter 1 verses 26 and 27: Then God said, *"Let Us make man in Our image, according to Our likeness; So God created man in His own image; in the image of God He created him; male and female He created them."*

God's infinite power is seen in everything because everything was created by Him. Think about this. Great creators of things-builders, sculptors, artists-are known by their works and they are recognized by what they have created. The great artist Thomas Kincade was and is known by his great paintings. You can look at a painting and know with very little education regarding the matter if the painting is a Kincade. No matter how much we want to be in denial, humanity instinctively knows that something far greater than man made everything.

What is the basic point that Satan attacks regarding God? It is God's infinite nature. By reducing God's nature to the finite, God becomes something finite and then there is no universal standard that can be the basis for standardized truths or morals. Therefore, since Satan convinced Adam and Eve that they could be like God, mankind has known deep down in his soul that there is a God. What did Adam and Eve do after they sinned when God came into the garden? They hid. Why? Because they knew they had sinned. God deniers are like every other denier in the world, they hide from the truth.

There are people who deny that the Holocaust ever took place despite the totality of evidence. There are deniers that the world was ever completely covered with water as indicated by Noah's flood despite the evidence. There are deniers that Jesus died and rose the third day despite the evidence. No matter how irrational your denial might be, if you really don't want something to be true in your life, just deny it.

We see it all the time in many ways. We are seeing major denial right now in politics and the Mainstream Media. Certain truths are coming out that don't fit their narratives, so they are pretending to be ostriches and stick their head in the sand. However, just because you deny the truth, reality or proof of something does not make it any less real. Saying that God does not exist, no matter how many billboards you put up, is not going to make it true. Even Christians who deny that God could have created in six days are not facing the reality of God's Word.

Do you realize that in the beginning man knew God? Man (Adam) walked and talked with the Almighty Creator. Knowing about God is not a case of evolutionary discovery. Man did not evolve from lower life forms and then decide that he needed some type of deity to worship. How could that idea have evolved in humankind when their ancestors the apes felt no need to worship anything? In fact, apes and every other animal act on instinct. They mate, they kill, they have no remorse, they don't feel guilty. How then is it that when we became mankind, that we knew instinctively that there was right and wrong, good and evil? Because mankind has known about God from the very beginning.

So, are we without remedy? John 3:16-17: *"For God so loved the world that He gave His only begotten Son, that whoever believes in Him should not perish but have everlasting life. 17 For God did not send His Son into the world to condemn the world, but that the world through Him might be saved."*

On Palm Sunday 2020, Pastor Greg Laurie of Harvest Church was sharing an online message because of the Covid-19 restrictions. He shared this the next day about a message he received on his Instagram flowing the service.

"Thank you, Pastor Greg. I have been an atheist for 15 years and lately I've been questioning everything. I saw on Facebook (FB) that the president said he was tuning into Greg Laurie so I decided to tune in and right when Greg said, someone is watching who is scared of death and doesn't know if they are right with God. I started to cry. I accepted Jesus into my heart. Thank you."

Jesus Christ is the remedy for eternity and that is what is most important, because it is going to last a really long time.

8 Hold On, A Message of Hope!

You know, every one of us in this life is searching for something, particularly in this time of medical, civil, and economic upheaval. We all want good health, safety, a better life, money, and the list goes on. For many people, this search has led them down some of the dark alleys of life into addictions and abuses. Many people are afflicted. The truth is that each and every human ever born on this planet has a problem from the very beginning of their lives. That problem is sin. When Adam and Eve fell for Satan's lie that they could be like Gods, they condemned all of humanity. Their sin also cursed the earth.

We all face a life of sin, and it is that sin that drives us to find a way out. Sometimes it's through alcohol or drugs, pornography, wild living, or one of a hundred other self-destructive activities that we use to mask the emptiness in our lives. Satan would like you to believe that there is this life, and that is all there is. But there is something that comes after this earthly life and that is called eternity. And the creator of the universe has created a way for us to fill that emptiness in our spirit and provide for us in eternity.

Have you ever heard the Rock and Roll song "Hold On"? I bet you didn't know that God can reach people through rock and roll. "Hold On" was the band Kansas' thirteenth single, eighth top one-hundred hit, and fifth top forty hit, peaking at #40. The song was first released on the 1980 album *Audio-Visions*, which was the last album recorded with the original band before Steve Walsh left. The song was written by Kerry Livgren, the founder of Kansas.

He wrote "Hold On" after accepting Jesus Christ as his Lord and Savior. He said he was thinking of his wife Vicki who had watched him go through quite a spiritual quest - and her salvation. Kerry says that his quest was long and hard. He knew that he needed something in his life but he didn't know what that was. What he was sure about was that he knew it couldn't be Christianity that he was seeking.

In his own testimony Kerry Livgren says that he explored every type of religion known to mankind but none of them seemed to do the trick, to fill that emptiness. During this same time, he watched as some members of the group in order to fill that same emptiness of spirit began to drink, do drugs, and live life large as they say.

Quoting from Wikipedia about Kerry Livgren, "In early 1979, Livgren became interested in *The Urantia Book,* a series of papers that claim to be a revelation authored by supernatural beings. Its influence can be felt in the lyrics of Kansas' 1979 album *Monolith.* Livgren subsequently rejected Urantia doctrine, and while on tour with the band in support of Monolith, he converted to Christianity. This was a result of a series of debates in the back of the tour bus with Jeff Pollard of Louisiana's Le Roux, the opening act for Kansas during the tour. The discussions between Livgren and Pollard concerned whether the Bible or the Urantia Book was the accurate record of the life of Jesus Christ. Because of the debates, Livgren became convinced that the Bible was the genuine record of Christ and that he had been mistaken in following the teachings of the Urantia Book. After a private hotel room conversion experience, he became an evangelical Christian."

That hotel room was in Indianapolis, Indiana right after the band had played there. Kerry says of that night about Christ and Christianity, "If this is true, then I don't care if I don't like it, I want the truth and at that moment I became somebody else."

Matthew 13: 10 -15: *"And the disciples came and said to Him, "Why do You speak to them in parables?" 11 He answered and said to them, "Because it has been given to you to know the mysteries of the kingdom of heaven, but to them it has not been given. 12 For whoever has, to him more will be given, and he will have abundance; but whoever does not have, even what he has will be taken away from him. 13 Therefore I speak to them in parables, because seeing they do not see, and hearing they do not hear, nor do they understand. 14 And in them the prophecy of Isaiah is fulfilled, which says: 'Hearing you will hear and shall not understand, And seeing you will see and not perceive; 15 For the hearts of this people have grown dull. Their ears are hard of hearing, And their eyes they have closed, Lest they should see with their eyes and hear with their ears, Lest they should understand with their hearts and turn, So that I should heal them."*

In the song "Hold On," we hear a call to hold on and how our tomorrow can be different from today. We also hear about what it was and can be like to be alone. Additionally there is a question about who you can run to. King David also had these thoughts as we read in Psalm 69:16-18: *"Hear me, O LORD, for Your loving kindness is good; Turn to me according to the multitude of Your tender mercies. 17 And do not hide Your face from Your servant, For I am in trouble; Hear me speedily. 18 Draw near to my soul, and redeem it; Deliver me because of my enemies."*

King David had been speaking of the spiteful reproaches which his enemies cast upon him. He pleads for God's mercy and truth because there is mercy in God, a multitude of mercies, all kinds of mercy, inexhaustible mercy, mercy enough for all, enough for each, and hence we must take our encouragement in praying. The truth also of His salvation (the truth of all those promises of salvation which He has made to those that trust in Him) is a further encouragement. *"Turn to me"*, according to the multitude of thy tender mercies. See how highly he speaks of the goodness of God: in him there are mercies, tender mercies, and a multitude of them. If we think well of God, and continue to do so under the greatest hardships, we need not fear because God will do well for us. He takes pleasure in those that hope in his mercy. Jesus is there when no one else is. He is waiting for your call and He will not turn away.

Revelation 3:20: *"Behold, I stand at the door and knock . If anyone hears My voice and opens the door, I will come in to him and dine with him, and he with Me."*

Are you standing on the brink? Are you feeling all alone? Your tomorrow can truly be different from your today. Just as Kerry Livgren discovered in that hotel room in Indianapolis, Indiana in 1979, all you have to do is answer the door of your heart and soul. You don't have to go looking for Christ, you don't have to call information for His number, you don't even have to Google Him.

Revelation 3:20; *"Behold, I stand at the door and knock . If anyone hears My voice and opens the door, I will come in to him and dine with him, and he with Me."*

As we have just read about, music has always been a great way to convey a message. Music can also do other things as we read here in 1 Samuel 16:23; *"And so it was, whenever the spirit from God was upon Saul, that David would take a harp and play it with his hand. Then Saul would become refreshed and well, and the distressing spirit would depart from him."*

It is obvious that God loves music since He gave it to His human creation. After all, what are the Psalms? Basically songs, many created and sung by King David. We know from the verse we just read that he was a very good musician.

Throughout the history of mankind, music has been used for many things; to stir up emotions from love to hate, from peace to war, and everywhere in between. In 1768, John

Dickinson of Delaware, the celebrated author of a series of essays entitled *The Farmer's Letters,* wrote to James Otis of Massachusetts, "I enclose you a song for American freedom. I have long since renounced poetry, but as indifferent songs are very powerful on certain occasions, I venture to invoke the deserted muses. I hope my good intentions will procure pardon, with those I wish to please, for the boldness of my numbers."

This was the first stanza of his song:

Come join band in hand, brave Americans all,
And rouse your bold hearts at fair Liberty's call;
No tyrannous acts, shall suppress your just claim,
Or stain with dishonor America's name.

Music is important for so many reasons. We sing songs of worship during church services, we even have virtual worship online. However, back in the late 1950s and the early sixties an evil and decadent form of music was raising up, and according to the grown-ups of the time, this music would lead to the destruction of the morals of America's youth. Yes, I am talking about Rock and Roll.

This is from Youth Culture in the 1950s, "During the 1950's many parents did not like Rock and Roll because they thought that it caused juvenile delinquency. At the time the music contained sexual connotations, this vulgarism and suggestive choice of words made the teens want to listen to it more because their parents did not approve, and teens felt like they had something to belong to. Many parents at the time gave their children ultimatums to stop listening to the music but it was unsuccessful. Parents feared that their children would start to act and dress like these musicians."

Truthfully, there was and is a lot of sex and drug innuendo in Rock and Roll music and it has gotten more blatant as the years have progressed. Question: Is there anything that God cannot reach into and have a presence if He so desires? No there isn't!

In 1965, December to be exact, the rock group The Byrds released a song right out of scripture; Ecclesiastes (3:1-8) Anyone know what that song was? "Turn! Turn! Turn!" It was on the charts for 14 weeks topping out at number 1. That's a lot of teenagers hearing the word of God straight from the Bible. In fact, the Scripture was listed on the record. I know this because I still have my originally purchased copy. Pete Seeger, who wrote the song, said that that section of scripture is a great poem.

However, these verses are more than just a great poem. Solomon is generally accepted as the writer of Ecclesiastes which is a book of wisdom dealing with the meaning of life. According to Dr. J, Vernon McGee, "many ungodly people also look to Ecclesiastes for foundational material for their worldly and secular beliefs."

What we primarily see here in these verses is that for everything there is a time, a season if you will. Just as we have been through the Covid-19 pandemic, the economic downturn, and the civil unrest, it will nonetheless end and complete their seasons. This is the truth of God from King Solomon who wraps up his writing in this book with verses 13 and 14 in chapter 12: *"Let us hear the conclusion of the whole matter: Fear God and keep His commandments, For this is man's all. 14 For God will bring every work into judgment, Including every secret thing, Whether good or evil."* Solomon concludes that what mankind needs to do is to fear God, not to be afraid of Him, but to keep His commandments, show reverence towards God and worship God.

In 1969, The Byrds in their album *"The Ballad of East Rider"* included the song "Jesus is Just Alright." This song was written by gospel singer Arthur Reid Reynolds. Following that, the Doobie Brothers released it first on an album in 1972 and then as a single in early 1973. The

Doobie Brothers were not Christian, but if God can speak through a donkey, He can certainly speak through Rock and Rollers. This was an interesting time to sing about what a friend Jesus is following what happened in 1972. The terrorist attack at the Munich Olympics, it was the peak of the anti-Vietnam war protests, the continuing battle between Great Brittan and the Irish Republican Army and there was the breaking of the Watergate scandal. Amidst all of that a song about how cool Jesus was, was playing on the rock and roll radios stations across America for 11 weeks. How cool was that!

I find it interesting that in times of great concern and apparent upheaval, God seems to send us messages of hope like this song also released in 1972 by Stephen Stills titled "Jesus Gave Love Away for Free." The third and final verse of the song seems to come right out of Genesis 2:21-24: *"And the Lord God caused a deep sleep to fall on Adam, and he slept; and He took one of his ribs, and closed up the flesh in its place. 22 Then the rib which the Lord God had taken from man He made into a woman, and He brought her to the man. 23 And Adam said: "This is now bone of my bones And flesh of my flesh; She shall be called Woman, Because she was taken out of Man." 24 Therefore a man shall leave his father and mother and be joined to his wife, and they shall become one flesh. "*

Jesus gave love away for free. Amen to that! Is that all we are to do regarding Jesus? We heard in the 1971 song by Ocean called "Put Your Hand in the Hand" of Jesus who is who we need to hold onto. In fact, the Reverend Billy Graham in his 1971 message "Who is Jesus" had this to say, "and nature obeyed Him and our young people believe that today because one of their top tunes at the moment is put your hand in the hand of the one who calmed the sea."

It is very interesting how many rock and roll songs that contained mentions of God or were just out right songs about God like the 1971 release by the group Black Sabbath, yes I know, it would seem to be a bit of an oxymoron, titled "After Forever" This song talks about your soul, can it be saved and more. Another song released in 1972 by the group Wishbone Ash who were not by their own statement a particularly Christian band, was this end times song titled "The King Will Come."

Do you see how God was and does reach out through the medium of Rock and Roll to reach people, particularly young people. Now that's not to say that there were not more than enough songs of evil, sex, anger, drugs and so on.

But my point is that God wanted a place in this medium and no one can keep Him out.

To end our stroll through God and Rock and Roll memories, how could we conclude better than with the 1969 release by the Edwin Hawkins Singers of "Oh Happy Day." Wikipedia has these comments regarding the song "Oh Happy Day". "It is a 1967 gospel music arrangement of an 18th-century hymn. Recorded by the Edwin Hawkins Singers, it became an international hit in 1969, reaching No. 4 on the US Singles Chart, No. 1 in France, Germany and the Netherlands and No. 2 on both the UK singles chart and Irish Singles Chart. It has since become a gospel music standard."

And isn't this a great way to end this chapter? Because if you are saved and Jesus Christ is your savior, it is a happy day! And it can be a happy day if you pray and accept Jesus Christ as your Lord and savior, the one who shed His blood so that we might have eternal life. Remember, on the other side of the door to eternity, there are only two people who'll be there to greet you. One is the root of evil and eternal punishment and the other is the King, Jesus Christ, with whom we will live in eternity with the crystal clear river of the water of life that John wrote about.

Turn back to the end of Chapter 2 for a prayer of Salvation.

9 Is It ME or HE

Isn't our culture great! I mean, talk about no worries, except for medical pandemics that ravage the world, massive civil unrest, and near economic disaster. But, even in the midst of these events and through these events, if something is wrong in your life, society says it's not your fault. Today's culture tells us that no matter what, we are ok, we are the best, it's all about me.

Did you know that if you do a Google search for the phrase "me generation" you will get over 15-million hits in less than five seconds? After all, this is the land of the free, and we are free to do what we want, as long as it doesn't hurt anyone else, unless they are unborn babies, but that doesn't count.

Like most everything else in America, today's culture has turned meaning on its head. Not only that, we as a culture have come to a place of self-worship: I need to look better, I need this or I need that, I'll do it, but how does it benefit ME! You see, in the world today there is a problem. We think everything is about us. I, ME, WE, SHE, HE, THEY, all of those miss the point. Does anyone know what the point is? It is all about God!

So, this leads us to a few questions.

1. Why do I exist as a person?

2. Why did God create me?

3. What should I be doing for God?

Pastor Rick Warren puts it this way in chapter one of his book *The Purpose Driven Life*, "It's not about you. The purpose of your life is far greater than your own personal fulfillment, your peace of mind, or even your happiness. It's far greater than your family, your career, or even your wildest dreams and ambitions. If you want to know why you were placed on this planet, you must begin with God. You were born by His purpose and for His purpose."

There are five Biblical mandates from God that I would like to touch on. Each on its own is worthy of lengthy consideration, but I want to highlight these five as a starting point to answer our questions about life while remembering who and what it is all about.

Let us begin at the beginning. When we are saved, we are newborn as a Christian. So as any newborn, we must what? Grow! We must have spiritual growth as we see in Colossians chapter 2 verses 6 and 7: *"As you therefore have received Christ Jesus the Lord, so walk in Him, 7 rooted and built up in Him and established in the faith, as you have been taught, abounding in it with thanksgiving."*

The Apostle Paul is encouraging the Colossians to go on as they had originally begun, and that was by Faith. The emphasis here seems to be on the word "Lord." In other words, they had acknowledged that in God there was complete sufficiency. God was enough, not only for Salvation, but for the whole of their Christian lives. Paul is urging them not to go astray by accepting the teachings of men, no matter how convincing they may sound. The word "walk" is one that is often used of the Christian life. It speaks of action and progress.

Paul uses an expression from agriculture, then one from architecture. The expression "rooted" refers to what took place at the time of our conversion. It is as if the Lord Jesus Christ is the soil and we find our roots in Him, drawing all our nourishment from Him. Paul also emphasizes the need to have our roots deep so that we can not be torn up by opposing winds. Next Paul uses the image of a building suggesting Jesus is the foundation of our strength and life.

But what do I need for spiritual growth? Well, here are some of the ingredients.

1. Faith is the first ingredient. Faith is necessary for salvation. Unsaved people cannot grow in the Lord because they do not have the first ingredient of saving faith.

2. Virtue is next. Moral goodness, right living, and saving faith will bring about right living.

And just in case you don't think that God doesn't care or pay attention, the Bible teaches otherwise.

3. Add some knowledge. You need knowledge of God, and the things of God in general. And you get this how?   Bible study and prayer.

4. Some temperance and self-control. Paul models this trait in 1 Corinthians 9:27: *"But I discipline my body and bring it into subjection, lest, when I have preached to others, I myself should become disqualified."*

5. Patience is next. It's the steadfastness of faith during trials and suffering. Patience works hand in hand with faith. It displays a restfulness and a peace during times of trials such as we have witnessed during the Covid-19 pandemic, civil unrest, and economic difficulties.

6. Godliness, this is reverence, seeking to conform to the mind of God in all things by the power of the Holy Spirit. Godliness involves a transformation in which we begin thinking as God thinks. We see sin as God sees sin. We see lost souls as God sees lost souls. We see all of life through a Godly world view.

7. Add brotherly kindness. A Christian should never be unkind to a fellow believer, or to a sinner.   Courtesy, genuine love and kindness are marks of a true Christian. We

witnessed an untold number of acts of kindness throughout the Covid-19 crisis.

As we grow, we also need to worship. God wants us to worship Him in everything we do, as we see in Psalm 34 verses 1 through 3: *"I will bless the LORD at all times; His praise shall continually be in my mouth. 2 My soul shall make its boast in the LORD; The humble shall hear of it and be glad. 3 Oh, magnify the LORD with me, And let us exalt His name together."*

Salvation from sin is a gift of such tremendous value that it should draw unceasing thanks from our hearts to the Giver. If God's praise were to be continually on our lips, we could not begin to exhaust the subject. And our boast of being saved must be in God alone. Plus, we should as King David did, worship God always and every way.

But as humans, we must be careful about what we worship, because we tend to become like what we worship. If we:

- Worship possessions...we can become a materialistic person.

- Worship money...we can become a greedy person.

- Worship sex...we can become a lustful person.

- Worship power...we can become a corrupt person.

- Worship Jesus...we become a more Christ like person.

Worship is service of God expressed, not only in religious gatherings, but also in every area of life. The life of worship requires obedience to God's Word despite feelings, or circumstances. It means holding on to God's truth no matter how heavy the burden or dark the day. Belief that the Lord provides enables the true worshipper to sacrifice without reservation. And why should we live this life of worship?? BECAUSE WE OWE IT TO GOD!

But as we grow and worship, we need to develop a passion for God and others. This passion will help us continue on with our Biblical purpose. Matthew 22 verses 37 through 40 says: *"Jesus said to him, " 'You shall love the LORD your God with all your heart, with all your soul, and with all your mind.' 38 This is the first and great commandment. 39 And the second is like it: 'You shall love your neighbor as yourself.' 40 On these two commandments hang all the Law and the Prophets."*

This means that man's first obligation is to love God with the totality of our being. And that means with all our heart, soul, mind, and body. Secondly, Jesus commanded us to love our neighbor. However, this is not just a passing fancy or something we when we are in the mood, we are to have a passion about these commandments.

124

Passion is a display of emotion such as love, joy, etc. It denotes strong feeling, fervor, enthusiasm and zeal. Passion is one of the key ingredients in a Christian's life. Not passion for worldly things, but a true heartfelt passion, desire, and fervor for Jesus. The type of passion that I am talking about is something that burns on the inside and consumes our thought processes, consumes our decision making, consumes our worship, consumes our emotions and our will. Passion is what takes a handful of scared Apostles and turns them into unwavering preachers for Christ!

I believe that many Christians today are lacking passion for Jesus. We have passion for our friends, family, things, even our pets, but where is our passion for God? When you were first saved, do you remember how great it felt? But where is that feeling, that passion, now? And if you are reading this and you are not yet saved, then pray with your heart for the Salvation through Jesus Christ.

"Dear God, thank you for sending Your Son, the Lord Jesus Christ, to pay for my sins on the cross. Thank you that He died for me. I acknowledge that I am a sinner and that I cannot save myself. Please forgive me all my sins. I receive your gift of salvation by faith. Thank you for loving me enough to save me. In Jesus' name, Amen."

As previously mentioned in chapter 2, if you prayed that prayer, I want to congratulate you on becoming a new member of the family of God. Additionally, I have something to send you from In The Beginning Ministries that will assist you as you move forward in your new justified walk with Jesus Christ. If you would, I would like you to email me at itbministries@gmail.com with your mailing address and say in the topic line, New Child of God. And don't worry, your email and address will only be used to send you the information that I just spoke about.

I believe that many of us pray, read the Bible, attend church, and serve the Lord out of obligation because we are supposed to. However, passion does not operate out of obligation. Passion operates as a result of agape love.

Passion loves and serves because it wants to, not because it has to. To paraphrase Dr. Albert Mohler from chapter three, Christians do what they do because they are Christians. Passion is serving God because there is nothing else that we would rather be doing. There is no passion without relationship. Passion is focused on a person or thing. Passion is energized by a person or thing. Knowing Jesus personally is essential to having a passionate relationship with Him.

But be advised, Satan will do everything in his power to keep you from that exciting relationship. Satan will tell you that you are being silly, or you are too vocal, or that you are making a spectacle of yourself. Satan will do anything he can to throw water on the fire of your passion for God. And if you don't think that's true, just look at what Christians are enduring today especially during the Covid-19 crisis when churches were closed, and Christians were forbidden sometimes under threat of arrest or citation, from gathering even in their cars.

However, the positive side of this is that it forced churches to go to the internet. What Satan meant for bad, God will always use for good. What we witnessed was millions of people who would not go to a church building that have ventured onto the internet church with the glorious result of thousands and thousands accepting Jesus Christ as their Savior.

As we have seen, part of showing that we are Christians is acting like one, which is easier when we are driven or passionate about it. Another way of showing our Christianity and fulfilling our Biblical purpose is service.

Isaiah 58 verses 6 through 12 tells us:

6 "Is this not the fast that I have chosen:
To loose the bonds of wickedness,
To undo the heavy burdens,
To let the oppressed go free,
And that you break every yoke?

7 Is it not to share your bread with the hungry,
And that you bring to your house the poor who are cast out;
When you see the naked, that you cover him,
And not hide yourself from your own flesh?
8 Then your light shall break forth like the morning,
Your healing shall spring forth speedily,
And your righteousness shall go before you;
The glory of the Lord shall be your rear guard.
9 Then you shall call, and the Lord will answer;
You shall cry, and He will say, 'Here I am.'
"If you take away the yoke from your midst,
The pointing of the finger, and speaking wickedness,
10 If you extend your soul to the hungry
And satisfy the afflicted soul,

Then your light shall dawn in the darkness,
And your darkness shall be as the noonday.
11 The Lord will guide you continually,
And satisfy your soul in drought,
And strengthen your bones;
You shall be like a watered garden,
And like a spring of water, whose waters do not fail.
12 Those from among you
Shall build the old waste places;
You shall raise up the foundations of many generations;
And you shall be called the Repairer of the Breach,
The Restorer of Streets to Dwell In.

Those who practice social justice or service are assured of guidance, healing, and protective escort. Your righteousness may mean the above-mentioned acts of mercy or it may mean the righteousness of God which is imputed to those who believe. The Godly one is assured that whenever they call, the Lord will answer "here I am" if the person will eliminate oppression, and stop pointing the finger in accusation or in scoffing and cease mud-slinging and slander.

Service is one of the mainstays of Christianity, the prime example of this comes from Christ Himself as He washed the feet of the Apostles. So, should we be willing to do any less? As an extension of service, we can easily move right into the Great Commission and evangelism. Matthew 28 verses 18 through 20 says: *"And Jesus came and spoke to them, saying, "All authority has been given to Me in heaven and on earth. 19 Go therefore and make disciples of all the nations, baptizing them in the name of the Father and of the Son and of the Holy Spirit, 20 teaching them to observe all things that I have commanded you; and lo, I am with you always, even to the end of the age." Amen."*

Jesus is saying that He now has all the authority as the head of the new creation, The key word here is "authority." In the Greek it is "*exousia* (ex-oo-see'-ah). It means the privilege, force, capacity, competency, freedom, delegated influence of complete authority, power, right, strength.

(Strong's Exhaustive Concordance of the Bible NT1849).

So with that authority, Jesus issues some marching orders. There are three specific orders in the Great Commission.

First: Go and make disciples of all the nations. The key operative here is to GO, not to gather in the church or just to support missions from far away, Jesus tells us to GO which means pretty much what is says.

Second: Baptize them in the name of the Father, Son and Holy Spirit. Once again, the responsibility rests on us as messengers for Christ to teach baptism and press it as a command.

Third: Teach them to observe all things that I have commanded. First off, that means that we have to observe all things that Jesus commanded, then we are commanded to pass that along to new believers. The essence of discipleship is seeking to become like the Master, and this is brought about by systematic teaching of and submission to the Word.

What are we, I, you doing to carry out the Great Commission? I don't know about you, but for me, this is easier said than done. A few years ago, Don Posterski wrote a book called *Why I am afraid to tell you I'm a Christian?* He says, "why are we afraid to tell people we are a Christian? IS IT MAYBE BECAUSE WE ARE AFRAID, WE WILL THEN HAVE TO ACT LIKE ONE?"

Do you think of evangelism as something that others are called to do? Do you feel like I could never be a Billy Graham or a Greg Laurie or even a Nick Vujicic. Well, here's a thought:

we are all called to be an evangelist but that does not mean that we have to change who we are. Remember, "God prepares the called, He doesn't call the prepared." We can be ourselves. God knew what He was doing when He made you and me. He gave us each our own unique personality and He wants us to use that in His service.

Effective evangelism flows out of a genuine, loving relationship with Christ. It is through this relationship that the Lord's love for lost people passes through us to others. If we have a personality change or a change in vocabulary or as soon as we begin to talk about spiritual matters with someone, it's hard to believe that we are genuine, so it becomes hard for the other person to believe that what we have to tell them is genuine.

I had to learn how to be genuine when I got into radio and television years ago. It is especially important if you are going to have people believe what you have to share. We also must realize that evangelism is a hands-on program. Jesus didn't fly over Jerusalem dropping Gospel tracts! No, He came and dwelt among us, eating and drinking with sinners. For people to get the message, someone must go and explain it to them. Just as words without actions are empty, so are some actions without words.

To be effective, we must not inappropriately rush or push a person. It takes time to understand the message, believe it, and act on it. Seldom do people hear the message for the first time and commit their lives to Christ. We must patiently bring people along, step by step. Evangelism does not necessarily mean that you have to go and bring people to Jesus. While there is no greater honor than to help a seeker find the Lord, we are evangelizing when we share God's word and His love, even if the other person does not make a decision at that moment. Remember, we might be at the beginning of this person's salvation chain, in the middle, or if we get to lead them to the Lord, the final link in the chain.

Saving a person is a team effort of the Holy Spirit and only God knows how many other people pass through a person's life sharing the truth about salvation with them. What we need to realize is that whenever anyone is saved, it is a miracle, and a miracle is God's business.

To wrap things up, we have a Biblical purpose for our existence here on earth. If we accept the gift of God's salvation, then we are expected to take some duties on board.

We are to grow our spirituality through prayer, Biblical learning and developing an ever-closer relationship with Jesus. As we grow, we are to worship God in everyway, every day with all our being. Remember, worshiping God is not just a Sunday morning event and it is not just songs. Worship can be and should be in everything you do, and you should be doing it for the Glory of God. From our worship we should develop a passion for God and others. A love that surpasses all other things. A focus for God and His Word that gives us joy in doing what God asks and not feeling that we are obligated.

Out of that passion and joy of working for God, we should be working to serve other people, by assisting them in whatever way the Holy Spirit guides us. Service is so Christ like, we should look for the opportunity every day.

So, no matter what part of the salvation chain we are to be a part of, we need to evangelize for God. We are called to do it and we need to do it. If you are a little afraid or embarrassed, just remember, do you want Jesus to be afraid or a little embarrassed to mention your name to His Father?

Evangelism is nothing more than sharing the Word of God and the gift of Salvation with others who might not hear that most important of information. I know that God is going to ask me why I didn't share His word with some people when I had the opportunity that He placed before me. That thought pains me more than I can share because I know that in that area, I have been disobedient and unfaithful in my life. I urge you to work to overcome any fear you might have about sharing the Word of God with others. Think about this, because I have; what if you are the last chance that person has for salvation?

So, what is the answer to the three questions I mentioned at the beginning?

Why do I exist as a person? For God's glory!

Why did God create me? For fellowship and worship!

What should I be doing for God? Spreading the word of His gift of eternal life.! Amen!

10 The Excitement of Jesus

As the song goes, "Jesus, Jesus, Jesus, sweetest name I know." Jesus was foretold in the book of Genesis chapter 3 verse 15: *"And I will put enmity Between you and the woman, And between your seed and her Seed; He shall bruise your head, And you shall bruise His heel."* We begin at the beginning with Adam and we can follow the line of Jesus through Scripture.

In 2 Samuel 7:12-13 God is speaking to David through the prophet Nathan:

"When your days are fulfilled and you rest with your fathers, I will set up your seed after you, who will come from your body, and I will establish his kingdom. 13 He shall build a house for My name, and I will establish the throne of his kingdom forever." While these verses are talking about David's son to be Solomon specifically, they are also talking about the Messiah. Many prophecies have a dual reference.

However, in the line of Jesus in the Old Testament there develops a bit of a little speed bump in Jesus' path to Earth. It comes from the prophet Jeremiah at the behest of Almighty God as Jeremiah relays a message in chapter 22, verses 24 through 30. Verse 30 is the speed bump: *"Thus says the Lord: 'Write this man down as childless, A man who shall not prosper in his days; For none of his descendants shall prosper; Sitting on the throne of David, And ruling anymore in Judah.'"*

This becomes really important, because Jesus had to fulfill two specific prophecies: one, Jesus had to be a blood descendant of David. Secondly, Jesus had to be legally entitled to sit on the throne of David. Additionally, He had to accomplish this while avoiding God's curse cutting off the royal line.

Someone might say that cutting off the royal line of David is more than just a little bump in the road for Jesus' path to Earth. How can Jesus descend from King David as Scripture says the Messiah will if the royal line has been cut off? Well that is a question I hope to answer to your satisfaction in this chapter.

You might know that there are two similar yet different genealogies of Jesus in the Gospels of Matthew and Luke. Matthew was writing for a Jewish audience and Luke was writing for a Gentile audience. Additionally, the Matthew genealogy of Jesus covers the royal line of King David, showing the Jews that Jesus did in fact fulfill the prophecies that the Messiah would come through the royal line of David. Dr. Luke on the other hand showed that Jesus was descended through the bloodline of King David through Mary.

There is an interesting note regarding Mary, *The Jewish New Testament Commentary* does not deal kindly with the New Testament translation of Jesus' mother's name. While we read the English translation Mary, in fact her Hebrew name was Miryam pronounced (meer-yawm'). *The Jewish New Testament Commentary* says this, *"This unfounded and artificial distinction produced by translators subtly drives a wedge between Yeshua's mother and her own Jewishness."* This westernizing of Miryam's Hebrew name takes away the etymology (which is the study of the origin of words and the way in which their meanings have changed throughout history) as it changed through translation to Mary. The first Miryam in the Bible was the sister of Moses, a prophet and a leader, a strong woman. And it would have to be a strong woman who would be the mother of the Messiah.

Think about what she faced as a young unwed pregnant girl betrothed to a man. Miryam faced the potential of not just being ostracized by the community and her relatives, but potentially could have been killed for such presumed and falsely accused sinful behavior. Yet it is through the bloodline of Miryam through Nathan the third oldest son of King David that Jesus' blood relationship to David the King is established, fulfilling one of the two requirements for Jesus to be the Messiah.

The other requirement for Jesus to be the rightful heir to the throne of David would have to come from the father. In this instance that means Joseph who is descended from Solomon. But what about the curse? That's an interesting question which I propose to answer.

While the royalty aspect of the line was ended at Jeconiah and his brother, Zedekiah, whose line was totally destroyed when he rebelled against Babylon and King Nebuchadnezzar. It is recorded in Jeremiah 52, verses 8 through 10: *"But the army of the Chaldeans pursued the king, and they overtook Zedekiah in the plains of Jericho. All his army was scattered from him. 9 So they took the king and brought him up to the king of Babylon at Riblah in the land of Hamath, and he pronounced judgment on him. 10 Then the king of Babylon killed the sons of Zedekiah before his eyes. And he killed all the princes of Judah in Riblah. 11 He also put out the eyes of Zedekiah; and the king of Babylon bound him in bronze fetters, took him to Babylon, and put him in prison till the day of his death."*

The line still continued as we see in the genealogy provided by Matthew. The non-royal line of David was established through the son of Jeconiah. The confirmation of the kingly side of the line of David is seen in Ezra 1:8-11: *"and Cyrus king of Persia brought them out by the hand of Mithredath the treasurer, and counted them out to Sheshbazzar the prince of Judah. 9 This is the number of them: thirty gold platters, one thousand silver platters, twenty-nine knives, 10 thirty gold basins, four hundred and ten silver basins of a similar kind, and one thousand other articles. 11 All the articles of gold and silver were five thousand four hundred. All these Sheshbazzar took with the captives who were brought from Babylon to Jerusalem."*

So, why did Ezra make mention of this Sheshbazzar and why did King Cyrus call him the prince of Judah and give him the property of the temple? That is because Sheshbazzar is the Babylonian name given to Zerubbabel, grandson of Jeconiah who continues the direct line to Joseph and to Jesus.

However the curse is still in place and the Messiah cannot come through an earthly descendant of the royal line of King David. God answers the conundrum by providing a miraculous birth. But wait, there is some consternation regarding the birth of Jesus. Since He is not the biological son of Joseph, then how could He legally inherit the throne of David?

It is through adoption. Is this Biblical? Yes it is. Moses was adopted by Pharaoh's daughter. Jacob adopted Joseph's sons Ephraim and Manasseh who would become two of the twelve tribes is Israel. Also, adopted sons could and did inherit the property of their fathers. Kingdoms are property.

Joseph was a descendant in the line of David through Solomon and Jeconiah. But, because of the curse could not be the biological father of the Messiah. However, he could and did adopt Jesus as his son. So, through adoption, Jesus was legally entitled to inherit the throne of David. And through His mother Mary, Jesus was a direct descendant in the bloodline of David through Nathan, thereby upholding the promise of Genesis 3:15: *"And I will put enmity Between you and the woman, And between your seed and her Seed; He shall bruise your head, And you shall bruise His heel."* He also fulfilled the covenants with Abraham, Isaac, Jacob and David.

Now we all know the whole "back story," as they call it, regarding the birth of Jesus the Messiah. Luke 2:1-11: *"And it came to pass in those days that a decree went out from Caesar Augustus that all the world should be registered. 2 This census first took place while Quirinius was governing Syria. 3 So all went to be registered, everyone to his own city. 4 Joseph also went up from Galilee, out of the city of Nazareth, into Judea, to the city of David, which is called Bethlehem, because he was of the house and lineage of David, 5 to be registered with Mary, his betrothed wife, who was with child. 6 So it was, that while they were there, the days were completed for her to be delivered. 7 And she brought forth her firstborn Son, and wrapped Him in swaddling cloths, and laid Him in a manger, because there was no room for them in the inn. 8 Now there were in the same country shepherds living out in the fields, keeping watch over their flock by night. 9 And behold, an angel of the Lord stood before them, and the glory of the Lord shone around them, and they were greatly afraid. 10 Then the angel said to them, "Do not be afraid, for behold, I bring you good tidings of great joy which will be to all people. 11* **For there is born to you this day in the city of David a Savior, who is Christ the Lord."**

Three final thoughts as this chapter draws to a close.

First, if nothing else, I hope this information helps to strengthen your faith in God, His Word and the truly miraculous way in which Jesus was brought to earth.

Secondly, some people wonder where Joseph is during the grown-up time of Jesus' life. Most Biblical theologians agree that Joseph dies between the time Jesus was 12 and when He was 30 and began His ministry. Why do we care? Because Joseph was in the line of King David's throne and for a son to inherit the throne, the father first had to pass away. Remember, Joseph was older than Mary when Jesus was born and after his passing, the way was clear for Jesus to ascend to the throne of David.

Thirdly, I want to emphasize just how powerful adoption is. Jesus legally inherited King David's throne through adoption. The Jews are God's chosen people through adoption. The Gentiles, when we are saved, are adopted into the family of Christ. As adopted sons and daughters of Christ, we are legally entitled to inherit the Kingdom of God. The Apostle Paul confirms this in Galatians 3:26-29: *"For you are all sons of God through faith in Christ Jesus. 27 For as many of you as were baptized into Christ have put on Christ. 28 There is neither Jew nor Greek, there is neither slave nor free, there is neither male nor female; for you are all one in Christ Jesus. 29 And if you are Christ's, then you are Abraham's seed, and heirs according to the promise."*

This should excite your soul, knowing that you can be adopted into the family of Jesus Christ. Now, are you adopted into God's family as a son or daughter? If not, your adoption is awaiting your acknowledgement of Jesus as your Lord and Savior. You can proclaim Him as your Lord and your Savior by prayer right where you are. Confess to Him your part in His death. Ask Him to forgive your sins and save you. Thank Him for His forgiveness. Tell someone else your decision, preferably by baptism in a Bible believing church.

11 The Supremacy of Jesus

Why is Jesus Supreme? Of course, Jesus is the Son of God, He is the Creator God, He is the redeemer, the one who came to earth as a sacrifice for the sins of Humanity.

Christopher Morgan, Ph.D. Dean, School of Christian Ministries and Professor of Theology at California Baptist University puts it this way in his book *Christian Theology* on page 223 "The Bible is the greatest story ever told, and God is the teller. The hero of the story is the Lord Jesus Christ. He is the Father's agent." That would seem to cover the short and sweet of it, but we shall drill deeper on this question of the Supremacy of Jesus.

Look at Hebrews 2:8-10: *"You have put all things in subjection under his feet." For in that He put all in subjection under him, He left nothing that is not put under him. But now we do not yet see all things put under him. 9 But we see Jesus, who was made a little lower than the angels, for the suffering of death crowned with glory and honor, that He, by the grace of God, might taste death for everyone. 10 For it was fitting for Him, for whom are all things and by whom are all things, in bringing many sons to glory, to make the captain of their salvation perfect through sufferings."*

We see that God the Father has put all things in subjection to Jesus. But as a human Jesus, we do not see all that Jesus is capable of in His Godly form since it was not His purpose to walk on the earth as God, but to walk on earth as a human. What we do see is a Jesus that was made a little lower than the Angels, like we humans were created. However, when you look at verse 10 you discover several things. One, it was fitting for Him, or in some translations it says it became Him. What was fitting or became Him? It means that this was what was intended for Jesus Christ in His person and purpose. Coming to Earth in human form to live life as a perfect example for others, then to be sacrificed for all the sins of humanity so that we might have a way to return to fellowship with God the Father, this is what is meant by it was fitting or became Him. And that would lead you to the next part of verse 10: *"for whom are all things and by whom are all things."* We know that all things were made by and for Jesus Christ. Jesus was the builder of all Creation, up to and including us.

We would next learn that it was God's intention from the beginning to provide a way for a return to fellowship with Him and humanity. When Adam and Eve sinned, God did not smack His forehead and exclaim "Oh Snap!" We see in John 3:17 God's plan for the sins of Adam and Eve and all humanity: *"For God did not send His Son into the world to condemn the world, but that the world through Him might be saved."* And by doing this, we

146

have the next step in verse 10*:" in bringing many sons to glory."* God's goal through Jesus was and is to bring as many to salvation as want to believe and partake in this incredible gift of eternal life.

What follows in verse 10 after Jesus brings many sons to glory? *"To make the captain of their salvation perfect through sufferings."* The Greek word translated here as captain also means a chief leader and Jesus was just that, the leader of salvation through His death on the cross. But unlike all others, after Jesus died, He did what? Jesus rose and saw the victory. The victory over sin, the victory over death, and the triumph of eternal life for those who would give themselves over to the Savior, Jesus Christ.

Next, we can take a look at verses 11 through 13 as we continue to call Captain my Captain, Jesus my Jesus, we also need to learn about the Supremacy of Christ. The first chapter of Hebrews shows us that Jesus is above the prophets and the angels. Why? Because the Creator is greater than the created. Let's look at verses 11-13: *"For both He who sanctifies and those who are being sanctified are all of one, for which reason He is not ashamed to call them brethren, 12 saying: "I will declare Your name to My brethren; In the midst of the assembly I will sing praise to You." 13 And again: "I will put My trust in Him." And again: "Here am I and the children whom God has given Me."*

Well the He who sanctifies is obvious, it is Jesus Christ. But who are those who are sanctified? The sanctified are only those people who are in Jesus Christ, who have accepted Him as their Savior and have therefore been justified through faith and have been regenerated. Not only that, but because of Jesus' perfect work on the cross, His sacrifice allows us to be seen by God through Him. John Phillips in his commentary on Hebrews puts it like this, "No doubt, as far as our state is concerned, there is much of which we need to be ashamed. But as far as our standing is concerned, it is perfect. Such is the magnificence of Christ's work that He can bring us into the presence of the angels, into the presence of the Father Himself, and say, 'These are my brethren.'"

But let's take a step back and look at Sanctification, what is it? Is it a one and done type of event like Salvation? Well, once we are saved, we are saved. But that in no way means that we can continue on in life as we did. True Salvation should lead us to a new way of life as we put off our old sinful ways and put on our new life, and that is where Sanctification comes in.

Sanctification is a personal event in that it is not corporately shared amongst a group. It is something that each one of us who are saved must work at and grow in. This is not something that is imputed to us like righteousness. Matthew Henry in his

Commentary on verse 11 says, "True believers are those who are sanctified, endowed with holy principles and powers, separated and set apart from mean and vile uses to high and holy uses and purposes; for so they must be before they can be brought to glory."

The Reverend Billy Graham was a great example of what we are discussing here regarding Sanctification because he lived a life of holiness. Even though the Reverend Billy Graham has been laid to rest and while he is in the presence of the one who had died for him, Billy Graham none the less leaves an incredibly rich legacy of faith and service behind him. I want to remind you of what Timothy Beougher from the Southern Baptist Theological Seminary wrote regarding Billy Graham.

7 Things that every Christian can learn from Billy Graham:

1. Billy Graham believed in the authority of Scripture.

2. Graham knew the power of prayer.

3. He knew the fullness of the Holy Spirit.

4. Billy Graham focused on the cross.

5. Graham promoted personal evangelism.

6. He prepared for the future.

7. He lived a life of holiness.

Is It Well With Your Soul?

Pastor Greg Laurie shared after Billy Graham's death that he was so honored to have gotten to be friends with Billy Graham and said that he was just the same in public as he was in private. Loving his Savior and working to portray that message in life each and every day. 1 Corinthians 1:30-31: *"But of Him you are in Christ Jesus, who became for us wisdom from God — and righteousness and sanctification and redemption — 31 that, as it is written, "He who glories, let him glory in the Lord."*

While God is the author of Sanctification, and Jesus is the deliverer of Sanctification through His sacrificial death and resurrection, it is the Holy Spirit that is our personal Sanctification trainer if you will. The Holy Spirit is the one who is in touch with us daily and guides us in what we are supposed to do, including growing more holy on our Sanctification path. This is a journey that does not end until we are made perfect in our heavenly form. However, we are commanded to grow in our holiness. How? By regular spiritual workouts with our personal spiritual trainer the Holy Spirit.

Here are some basic spiritual workout tips; called L.O.R.P.

1. Lift - lift up the Bible in your hands.

2. Open - open the Bible.

150

3. **Read** - read Scripture on a daily basis and through that learn and grow.

4. **Pray** - pray daily, for yourself and your growth in the Lord. Pray for others. Pray for our nation and the unsaved here and around the world.

This daily workout, like a physical workout, will help you to build and strengthen your spiritual muscles. If you are serious about growing in your Sanctification, then you need to stop being a 90-pound spiritual weakling and get buffed in the spirit. It is God from whom all things flow. Salvation is from God. Justification is from God. Mercy is from God. Grace is from God. Sanctification is from God. And that is how He (Jesus) who sanctifies, and we who are being sanctified become one in the family of God. And because of this, the Bible tells us what happens in Hebrews 2, verse 11; *"for which reason He is not ashamed to call them brethren."*

You might remember the story of Joseph, so loved by his brothers that they sold him into slavery to a caravan headed to Egypt. From there Joseph goes through many trials but eventually ends up as second only to the Pharaoh in command of Egypt. When Joseph is reunited with his brothers who were all shepherds, a job that was disliked and looked down on by Egyptians, Joseph was nonetheless proud of his brothers and took them and introduced them as his brothers to the Pharaoh himself.

In the movie *Crocodile Dundee*, yes I am dating myself a bit, there is a scene where Mick is explaining to the reporter about how he had survived the crocodile attack, if he thought he was going to die, and if he was afraid of dying. "I read the Bible once. You know God and Jesus and all them Apostles? They were all fishermen, just like me. Yep. It's straight to heaven for Mick Dundee. Yep. Me and God... We be mates." Now as far as understanding salvation, Mick is a bit off, but I use this quote to illustrate that Jesus is not afraid to call those who are saved and sanctified His brethren. He is our mate. Now I am not saying that we are to get chummy with Jesus, because He is our Lord and we owe Him the respect He deserves, but from His viewpoint we certainly could be mates with Him in the family of God.

In fact we see that not only is Jesus not ashamed to call us brethren, He goes even further in Hebrews 2 verse 12: *"saying: "I will declare Your name to My brethren; In the midst of the assembly I will sing praise to You."* This is a quote by the author from Psalms 22 which is considered to have Messianic importance. Read verse one in Psalm 22, and see if it might be familiar: *"My God, My God, why have You forsaken Me?"* Yes, these are the same words uttered by Jesus on the cross. All of Psalm 22, though written by King David has nothing to do with his real life and can only be prophetical in nature alluding to the Messiah. The quote used in Hebrews 2 verse 12 is from Psalm 22 verse 22: *"I will declare Your name to My brethren; In the midst of the assembly I will praise You."*

The author has harkened back to Psalm 22 to make a connection for their listeners and readers, primarily Jews/Hebrews, showing them the connection of Jesus from the Old Testament prophecy of David to the actual event here in New Testament times. But the message was the same. David in his joy proclaimed the name of God, to the Jews of his day, and Jesus in His turn proclaimed the Name of God to those believers, primarily Jews but also some Gentiles after his death and resurrection.

However, the author of Hebrews wants to solidify his point regarding Jesus and His relationship with those who believe and have been saved through faith in Jesus Christ. So the author moves on from Psalm 22 to either Psalm 18 verse 2 or Isaiah 8 verses 17 and 18 depending on which Biblical commentator you read. But for the first part of verse 13, whether from Psalm or Isaiah, the point is that the believer is putting their trust in God, which is what the Author of Hebrews is saying of Jesus.

Look at the first part of Hebrews 2 verse 13: *"And again: "I will put My trust in Him."* The conjunction here in verse 13 translated "and again" basically means furthermore. Look at verse 12 and the beginning of verse 13 with the

Greek meaning; *"saying: "I will declare Your name to My brethren; In the midst of the assembly I will sing praise to You."* 13 *Furthermore: "I will put My trust in Him."*

Through a variety of verses in the New Testament, we find that Jesus was obedient to and trusted God the Father. So, Jesus here is not only willing to call those of us who are saved and sanctified His brethren, He is also telling us that He has placed His trust in the Father, and so should we. In fact, how much did Jesus trust His Father? He submitted to His own sacrifice, the reason He was here on earth in human form. Remember verses 9 and 10: *"But we see Jesus, who was made a little lower than the angels, for the suffering of death crowned with glory and honor, that He, by the grace of God, might taste death for everyone. 10 For it was fitting for Him, for whom are all things and by whom are all things, in bringing many sons to glory, to make the captain of their salvation perfect through sufferings."*

It was fitting for Jesus to come to Earth, to live on Earth, to teach on Earth, and to die and be resurrected on Earth in order to provide the sacrifice needed by humanity to be forgiven by God, but in all these things. Jesus always had trust in God the Father and, by His example, so should we.

Look at the second part of verse 13, *"and again or [furthermore]: "Here am I and the children whom God has given Me."* In Isaiah chapter 8 verse 18, the Prophet is saying that he will wait for and trust the Lord while waiting with those that the Lord has entrusted to the prophet's ministry, the God believing remnant of Judah. But here in Hebrews, the author is using the quote from Isaiah to show the New Testament Jews that Jesus, the crucified and risen Messiah, stands with those who have believed on Him. And those who believe have been given to Jesus Christ by the Father as Jesus is the head of the family of believers.

What we have here in verses 11 through 13 is Jesus who sanctifies the believers who are all in the family of God. Because of that, Jesus is not ashamed to call us brethren. Not only that, Jesus will declare God's name to the believers of the family of Christ. Furthermore, Jesus will place His trust in the Father as we also should. Additionally, Jesus is here amongst the family of believers that God has given to Him through their deliverance and Sanctification.

12 Is it Well With Your Soul?

Many things can affect us on a daily basis, sometimes minute to minute that can cause us to question "is it well with my soul"? Here on earth, as you are well aware, every day is not heaven. We all have trials and situations that cause either happiness or sadness or something in between. Even as a Pastor, I have struggled at times as to whether or not it was well with my soul. You might ask what is the "what" that I am talking about when I use the phrase "is it well with my soul?" Is it spiritual, physical, emotional, financial, relationships, what is it? Well, in my opinion it can be anything that causes us to lose the glory of our spiritual self. The Covid-19 pandemic, the economic problems, and the civil unrest that we have experienced are sad examples of something beyond our control that can tax our wellness in every way I just mentioned.

My soul, spirit, and person sustained the most continual attack that I can recall during the months of September through November 2018. I was leading a church as the Senior Pastor and had to help the congregation consider a merger with a larger church. When I was first told about the proposal, I consented to pray about it with my wife. After more than a week, we both concluded that this was what God desired to do with our church.

Our church, Unified Baptist Church in San Bernardino, California had been a declining church since before I was called to be their Senior Pastor in 2013. In fact, before I was called, the church had considered whether to close or to try to continue. They chose to try to continue and that began the search for a new pastor, me. We tried many times over the years to reach out to the community, to grow the church, but the efforts never seemed to take. But during all this time, the Lord always made sure that we had what we needed to survive and keep the church in operation.

I began to feel that God was keeping the church alive in order to take care of His property until He decided what to do with it. To me, the merger proposal was the proof that God did in fact have a greater plan for the property. The merger was completed by the end of 2018. I continually pray that God through the merger will use the property for great and mighty works.

However, there is a question that I would like to ask you. Is it well with Your Soul? Throughout this book I have attempted to share through some of my messages over the years how Jesus Christ can and does make it well with our souls. The great poem by Horatio G. Spaford that became the timeless hymn "It Is Well with My Soul" has this important reminder about life "when peace like a river attendeth my way; when sorrows like sea billows roll: Whatever my lot Thou hast taught me to say, it is well with my soul." Those words acknowledge an obvious truth. Life is a mixed bag, a hodgepodge of good and bad, of joy and sadness, of tragedies and treasures. The great King Solomon, son of King David wrote about these very thoughts in Ecclesiastes 3:1-8:

To everything there is a season, A time for every purpose under heaven:
2 A time to be born, And a time to die; A time to plant, And a time to pluck what is planted;
3 A time to kill, And a time to heal; A time to break down, And a time to build up;
4 A time to weep, And a time to laugh; A time to mourn, And a time to dance;
5 A time to cast away stones, And a time to gather stones; A time to embrace, And a time to refrain from embracing;
6 A time to gain, And a time to lose; A time to keep, And a time to throw away;
7 A time to tear, And a time to sew; A time to keep silence, And a time to speak;
8 A time to love, And a time to hate; A time of war, And a time of peace.

By the way, have you ever wondered what exactly a sea billow is? A sea billow is a large wave or swell of water, a great swell, surge or undulating mass. Just think of the ocean driven by a large hurricane and you have the idea.

Romans, chapter 8 is just what we need amid the uncertainties of life that we face.

In this section of verses the Apostle Paul is writing about the Glory that the believer will experience as part of our inheritance from God. But to deal with all that is going on in the world and our lives, we first need perspective. Look at verse 18: *"For I consider that the sufferings of this present time are not worthy to be compared with the glory which shall be revealed in us."* Perspective is defined as; "a particular way of viewing things that depends on one's experience and personality or "the ability to consider things in relation to one another accurately and fairly." (dictionary.cambridge.org)

Think of it this way, suppose that you receive a month's free vacation at a fabulous resort. But to get there you encounter a stretch of rough, bumpy dirt road. Would you get fed up and say "that's it! I'm sorry we ever started on this trip," probably not. I would say that most if not all of us would probably say something like, "this is a bit aggravating, but I'm not going to let it diminish the joy of our month-long vacation." However, in reality, how many of us fall into the trap of losing perspective? It is so easy to do so today, when nearly everything you hear or read in the news is negative. What can you do when you feel that you have lost perspective? You need to pray for the Holy Spirit to clean the spiritual lenses of your perspective glasses so you can see more clearly. We can see why in the words of the Apostle Paul in 2 Corinthians 4:16-18: *"Therefore we do not lose heart. Even though our outward man is perishing, yet the inward man is being renewed day by day. 17 For our light affliction, which is but for a moment, is working for us a far more exceeding and eternal weight of glory, 18 while we do not look at the things which are seen, but at the things which are not seen. For the things which are seen are temporary, but the things which are not seen are eternal."*

To better zero in on a good perspective, we need patience. But as many would attest to, myself included, patience is not always in plentiful supply. You might recall the phrase, "Lord grant me patience and do it right now." When the slings and arrows of the real world and the spiritual world all seem to be aimed at you, it is very hard to remain patient. In the movie *"13 Hours"* about the attack on Americans in the Libyan city of Benghazi, the CIA annex is about to be attacked. The U.S. defenders are waiting as the enemy creeps ever closer to their location, but one of the defenders keeps reminding the others to "let them come," let them get closer so that when the shooting started the defenders would have a better advantage. I am sure that was not easy to do, to watch and wait for the enemy to get closer. Often times, we face the same concern. The enemy is getting closer and we might even pray, "Lord, what are You waiting for?" The Lord being a "just in time" God is always waiting for the moment that best displays what He wants us to understand.

Let's look at Romans 8:19-24: *"For the earnest expectation of the creation eagerly waits for the revealing of the sons of God. 20 For the creation was subjected to futility, not willingly, but because of Him who subjected it in hope; 21 because the creation itself also will be delivered from the bondage of corruption into the glorious liberty of the children of God. 22 For we know that the whole creation groans and labors with birth pangs together until now. 23 Not only that, but we also who have the first fruits of the Spirit, even we ourselves groan within ourselves, eagerly waiting for the adoption, the redemption of our body. 24 For we were saved in this hope, but hope that is seen is not hope; for why does one still hope for what he sees?"*

There is some debate as to what Paul is talking about here, people or the Earth. Most Biblical scholars believe that Paul is in fact talking about the Earth and creation. Remember that in Genesis chapter 3 verse 17, God cursed the earth because of Adam's disobedience. The world and all that is in it has suffered greatly from the curse and Paul is saying here that not only we who are saved are looking forward with anticipation of God's coming, but so is the rest of creation. Look again at verse 20 and 21, but read it as one sentence: *"For the creation was subjected to futility, not willingly, but because of Him who subjected it in hope; because the creation itself also will be delivered from the bondage of corruption into the glorious liberty of the children of God."*

We are in the groaning period of Earth's time span, but better days arc coming. Eternity is ahead and is that not the real gift of God, to live with Him in eternity?

But we must have patience. Easier said than done isn't it? Bishop George Horne wrote "Patience is the guardian of faith, the preserver of peace, the cherisher of love, the teacher of humility. Patience governs the flesh, strengthens the spirit, stifles anger, extinguishes envy, subdues pride; she bridles the tongue, refrains the hand, tramples upon temptations, endures persecutions, consummates martyrdom. Patience produces unity in the church, loyalty in the state, harmony in families and societies; she comforts the poor and moderates the rich; she makes us humble in prosperity, cheerful in adversity, unmoved by calumny and reproach; she teaches us to forgive those who have injured us, and to be the first in asking forgiveness of those whom we have injured; she delights the faithful, and invites the unbelieving; she adorns the woman, and improves the man; is loved in a child, praised in a young man, admired in an old man; she is beautiful in either sex and every age.

Patience is clothed in the robes of the martyrs and in its hand it holds a scepter in the form of a cross. It rides not in the whirlwind and stormy tempest of passion; but its throne is the humble and contrite heart, and its kingdom is the kingdom of peace."

Creation is looking back as are we to the ideal conditions that existed in Eden before the Fall. But this is where patience becomes necessary. Creation was created out of God's spoken word and it is therefore important to Him. But mankind was created in the image of God and God does not want for anyone to perish in sin because we are very important to Him, so He is patient.

Can you be as patient as God? Probably not. But we can try to be a bit more patient, to have a little more understanding with those who disagree with us, with fellow believers who do not seem to understand Scripture as we do, with family to do the right thing at the proper time. It is distressing how little patience is shown by humanity. Social media, especially Twitter, has become the weapon of the lack of patience. Someone makes a comment and, almost instantly, supporters and adversaries respond, oftentimes with mean and hateful retorts that should never see the light of day.

Sadly, many people who do respond with immediate invective instead of taking a moment to reflect, showing little patience, ultimately regret what they wrote or said.

The following words are the advice of George MacDonald who died in 1905. He was a minister and novelist and reportedly inspired or mentored such novelists of his day like C.S. Lewis, J.R.R. Tolkien and The Reverend Charles Lutwidge Dodgson. You might recognize the Reverend's pen name of Lewis Carroll, the author of *Alice in Wonderland*. It is said that because of MacDonald's enthusiastic reception of the book by his three daughters, that Macdonald convinced Carroll to submit *Alice* for publication and as they say, the rest is history. This is what MacDonald says about patience: "Learn these two things: never be discouraged because good things get on so slowly here, and never fail daily to do that good which lies next to your hand. Do not be in a hurry, but be diligent. Enter into the sublime patience of the Lord. Be charitable in view of it. God can afford to wait; why cannot we, since we have Him to fall back upon? Let patience have her perfect work, and bring forth her celestial fruits. Trust to God to weave your little thread into a web, though the patterns show it not yet."

So as we wait for the coming of the Lord, we have perspective and patience, but we need to add providence. Look at Romans 8:25-30: *"But if we hope for what we do not see, we eagerly wait for it with perseverance. 26 Likewise the Spirit also helps in our weaknesses. For we do not know what we should pray for as we ought, but the Spirit Himself makes intercession for us with groanings which cannot be uttered. 27 Now He who searches the hearts knows what the mind of the Spirit is, because He makes intercession for the saints according to the will of God.*

28 And we know that all things work together for good to those who love God, to those who are the called according to His purpose. 29 For whom He foreknew, He also predestined to be conformed to the image of His Son, that He might be the firstborn among many brethren. 30 Moreover whom He predestined, these He also called; whom He called, these He also justified; and whom He justified, these He also glorified."

Something that struck me in studying these verses were the words of Dr. J. Vernon McGee in his commentary on verse 25 he writes, "you see, faith, hope, and love are the vital parts of the believer's life. There would be no hope if all were realized. Someday hope and faith will pass away with realization. In fact, both faith and hope will pass away in the glory which shall be revealed in us. Only love will abide."

Paul is pointing out that God does not leave praying and intercession up to us. God has provided help in the Holy Spirit. Have you ever had the feeling that you need to pray but were unsure of what it was that you needed to pray for or about? The Holy Spirit will pray for us when we may not know what to pray for, but we just know that we have to pray. Anyone other than me ever have that feeling?

Many times, verse 28 is misused as something we tell people who have suffered some tragic event in their lives. Because how do you answer their next question, which will be something like how will God use the death of my loved one for good or how will He use for good the near total destruction of our town like happened to the northern Californian town of Paradise on November 8th, 2018 to a raging wildfire. I would caution you not to use this verse in those types of situations. And in fact, while God will use the events in our lives for a purpose, the eventual good that God provides is an eternity with Him.

By the way, I am not going to deal with the predestination issue in these verses. That is for another time, but I will say that some believe that this is proof that God has already determined who is and is not going to Heaven. I believe with a great many others that God has predestined that anyone who accepts Jesus Christ as their Lord and Savior and asks for their sins to be forgiven is going to Heaven. And to me, that is the Providence that we are talking about, not the television show. Providence can be defined this way; "a looking to or preparation for the future, skill or wisdom in management, the care or benevolent guidance of God or nature."

This story is not mine, but makes a great point. Some years ago a vessel lay calm on a smooth sea in the vicinity of an iceberg. In full view the mountain mass of frozen splendor rose before the passengers of the vessel, its towers and pinnacles glittering in the sunlight, and clothed in the enchanting and varied colors of the rainbow. A party on board the vessel resolved to climb the steep sides of the iceberg, and spend the day in a picnic on the summit. The novelty and attraction of the hazardous enterprise blinded them to its danger, and they left the vessel, ascended the steep mountain of ice, spread their table on the summit, and enjoyed their dance of pleasure on the surface of the frosty marble. Nothing disturbed their security, or marred their enjoyment. Their sport was finished, and they made their way down to the water level and embarked. But scarcely had they reached a safe distance before the loud crash of the crumbling mass was heard. The scene of their gaiety was covered with the huge fragments of the falling pinnacles, and the giant iceberg rolled over with a shock that sent a thrill of awe and terror to the breast of every spectator. No one in that party could ever be induced to try that rash experiment again. But what is this world, with all its brilliance, with all its hopes and alluring pleasures but a glittering iceberg, melting slowly away? Its false splendor, enchanting to the eye, dissolves; and as drop after drop trickles down its sides, or steals unseen through its hidden pores, its very foundations are undermined, and the steady decay prepares for a sudden catastrophe. Such is the world. Too many who dance over its surface, and in a false security, forget the treacherous footing on which they stand. But can anyone who knows what it is avoid feeling that every moment is pregnant with danger, and that the final catastrophe is hastening on?

Sounds like a pretty good description of human society today, wouldn't you agree? This is why providence, believing that Jesus Christ is preparing us for eternity in Heaven is so important. While for the unsaved, their providence is preparing for an eternity apart from God.

Now we have perspective, patience, and providence. Finally we must have praise

Let's read Romans 8:31-39: *"What then shall we say to these things? If God is for us, who can be against us? 32 He who did not spare His own Son, but delivered Him up for us all, how shall He not with Him also freely give us all things? 33 Who shall bring a charge against God's elect? It is God who justifies. 34 Who is he who condemns? It is Christ who died, and furthermore is also risen, who is even at the right hand of God, who also makes intercession for us. 35 Who shall separate us from the love of Christ? Shall tribulation, or distress, or persecution, or famine, or nakedness, or peril, or sword? 36 As it is written: "For Your sake we are killed all day long; We are accounted as sheep for the slaughter." 37 Yet in all these things we are more than conquerors through Him who loved us. 38 For I am persuaded that neither death nor life, nor angels nor principalities nor powers, nor things present nor things to come, 39 nor height nor depth, nor any other created thing, shall be able to separate us from the love of God which is in Christ Jesus our Lord."*

Romans chapter eight ends with a praise of worship and that attitude should infuse us with a triumphant joy. Paul here is reflecting on the confidence that believers can have from the assurances that he has outlined in chapters 5 through 8. Using the questions in verses 31 through 35, Paul invites the reader to join in the celebration. In verse 36, Paul quotes from Psalm 44:22, showing that God's chosen have always faced opposition from the ungodly. In verse 37 Paul says that we are more than conquerors. In fact, we are also the victors through Christ who saved us. AMEN!

Then Paul tells us that he is persuaded which means he KNOWS. Paul is certain, there is no doubt in his mind that death cannot separate us from God, in fact it will take us into God's presence. When talking about neither height nor depth, these words back in biblical times, were used to denote the celestial space above and below the horizon. This means that nothing above or on or in the earth can separate believers from God.

In the movie *Cool Hand Luke* (shows you how old I am), the prison warden is fond of saying "What we have here is a failure to communicate." But just the opposite is true in Romans chapter 8. In fact, what we have here is a way to communicate by maintaining our perspective, while being patient, as we rely on the providence of God whom we need to praise in all that we do.

I would like to Quote Dr. McGee again as this book draws to a close; "My friend, salvation is a love story. We love Him because He first loved us. Nothing can separate us from that. We entered this chapter with no condemnation; we conclude it with no separation; and in between all things work together for good. Can you improve on this friend? This is wonderful!"

So, when peace like a river attends our way, when sorrows like sea billows roll, take time to read Romans chapter 8 and then say, **"it is well, it is well with my soul."**

www.ingramcontent.com/pod-product-compliance
Lightning Source LLC
LaVergne TN
LVHW011329080426
835513LV00006B/255